This Land
I Have Loved

by

Robert C. Balfour, Jr.

1887–1979

Per copy $17.50

2

FOREWORD

"THIS LAND I HAVE LOVED" tells the story of the area between Thomasville, Georgia, and Tallahassee, Florida, and includes a section near Albany, Georgia, when referring to the Georgia-Florida Field Trial Club activities.

Eighty-seven years have passed since I was born in Thomasville. For so long have I felt a strong inspiration to care for and improve our forests, as well as enjoy the outdoor sports they provide, that I sometimes think I must have been born with it. In addition to the beautifully wooded areas, irregularly dotted with fields both large and small, the many lakes, the rivers, and the nearby Gulf of Mexico all combine to make this location attractive.

Only a few persons are around now who witnessed, well before the turn of the century, the several large winter hotels in Thomasville operate to capacity with some of the nation's wealthiest and most prominent people as guests. Then Florida became the fashionable wintering place and finally the hotels were forced to close. However, many of the guests had acquired large tracts of land nearby which they gradually developed into superb hunting preserves, while at the same time carefully following the best husbandry practices of farming and forestry. These endeavors, combined with those of the local citizens, who, almost to the man—and often, the woman—love to fish and hunt, have created a vast area where preference is given to retaining the natural environment and where wildlife truly abounds.

When I started to write this book I had no idea that it would require five years, but I freely admit it was a work of love. Nor did I dream I would call on scores of persons for information and help. No one refused—when I explained my purpose everyone responded liberally and enthusiastically. I am indebted to all, and to some especially.

I started out with very definite scenes for illustration in mind, but never could I have got the pictures except for Tidwell's Studio. They simply kept shooting until a picture came out right, and I leave the measure of quality and artistry to the reader's judgment. Leo Miller went to great trouble in taking pictures of the Aucilla River and in getting the names of the islands in Lake Iamonia from the few old boatmen still alive.

The Thomasville Public Librarians looked up old pamphlets and books dealing with the dawning history of our section. Richard Tift, Herschel Clay and Bill Shealey filled me in with data, names, dates, etc., which only they could supply. Frank Eidson and Bill MacIntyre dug way back into their memories for facts about Dr. MacIntosh and somehow unearthed a tintype of the first golf professional of Glen Arven Country Club.

Mrs. Evelyn Yawn, an efficient worker in our office who also finds time to act as my secretary, typed and re-typed the manuscript from my scribbling and jotting. She stayed with it all the way, including its assembly and production. When I would slack up on my work, she pushed me on. Thanks, Evelyn, you were great.

I am almost sorry this book is finished because Thurman Scott, a good friend, has encouraged and advised me so many times while it was being written. Then he edited and assisted with the final form. I may have to write another book just to keep in touch with him! Thanks so much, Scotty.

Finally, to my beloved wife, Deborah, who, most of all, through your kindness, patience, love and inspiration spurred me on to the completion of this book, my eternal thanks.

Robert C. Balfour Jr.

CHAPTER ONE

All my long life I have worked in the woods. Studying and marking the trees, watching the wildlife, minding the weather and the elements all served to make me deeply conscious of God's great creation.

I will never forget cruising a stand of virgin longleaf timber on a brilliant, windy day in March of 1910. In no hurry, I stopped to listen to the musical sighing of the wind in the long needles high above, and to watch the colorful trunks sway from side to side. Occasional prolonged gusts would bend and strain them so far I marveled that they did not snap.

Then, unaccountably, my gaze was drawn to the ground, to a washed crevice where lay a perfectly shaped arrowhead, polished by the rain and bleached by the sun until it glowed. While admiring the arrowhead in the palm of my hand, it seemed to become even more beautiful. I forgot about my work, for events of centuries ago were racing through my mind.

How long ago was the arrow shot? Did it miss its target? Likely it did that time, I guessed, and likely the hunter searched for it in the dense wiregrass long and hard. Surely such a fine specimen would not be abandoned readily.

What kind of a man was the Indian who shot the arrow? Like me, a woodsman—he made his living in the woods, only far more completely than I. Did he enjoy the beauty of this forest and delight in filling his lungs with its clean, fresh air as I did? He must have found the area to his liking as otherwise it would have been a simple matter for him to move on to another.

How had this forest looked then? About the same as now, I reckoned, certainly not much different. Unlike so many tracts of woodland which lately had been stripped of trees and allowed to grow up in scrub oak and brush, it had been well managed. Such preservations called for an owner who looked beyond today, as every one of the huge pines was worth much money if felled for lumber.

The arrowhead was so perfectly shaped that it must have been chipped out of flint by a talented sculptor, and I wondered how long it had taken him. No doubt he was highly respected and esteemed by the tribesmen since the arrow tip was their chief means of getting food. What a hardy race of people the Indian were, I reflected—highly developed athletically, living entirely off the land, their "houses" made of animal skins stretched over poles, their medicines extracted from herbs and roots and bark. And what a pity that more of their knowledge and resourcefulness had not been handed down!

Nowadays, of course, Indians are looked upon with much more fairness and kindness. But back then, we were led to believe they were only cruel savages, not quite human, who somehow were in the wrong for defending their lives and their homeland. It was that concept that bothered me as I forgot about timber cruising and sat on the trunk of a fallen tree.

I turned the arrowhead first one way and then the other in my hand, my thoughts on its first owner, on the craftsman who made it, and on the people who long ago lived in these forests which were still abundant with game. Surely America was large enough for us all, and if a greater effort had been made to learn the Indians' culture the two races might well have lived in peace and harmony. That would have taken patience and compassion, of course, but how much better than forcibly wresting away their land and trying to wipe them out.

After a long while I got up, placed the arrowhead in my leather pocketbook and went about the timber cruising. This new possession had taken on a special significance for me.

Not long afterward I learned that not all the historians and chroniclers of early America were malevolent toward Indians. In 1765 when William Bartram traveled through Georgia and Florida, he wrote that he found the Indians leading a cheerful, prosperous life in a peaceful village of Seminoles under their wise chief. He told of dashing, thundering feats of horsemanship by the young men, half-naked on their spirited Spanish horses, of the cattle, pigs, orange trees and beautiful gardens, and of feasts by the fires. He said the Seminoles were superior and brave men, magnanimous and religious, living by their own ancient laws.

Bartram described the Seminoles as large, copper-skinned men with small, charming wives, and said they were devoted to their well mannered children. He wrote of them realistically, as affectionate, honest and loyal

to their friends and allies, and at once capable of jealousy and cruelty to their enemies.

We know that Indians had lived for thousands of years on their land. It was their temple—they worshiped in the open, watched the seasons come and go, the trees bud and

bear fruit, the wild animals mate and care for their young. In the most natural way on earth they witnessed God's creation unfold before their very eyes.

After the white man came the temple was quickly torn down as the Indians were forced to sign treaties which ran them out, all for little money and many promises of protection. After they had relinquished rights to 35 million acres of the finest land in the south, their leader was quoted as saying, "Our white brothers cry out against us when we will not give them more land."

As the records witness, all the treaties were broken and the promises unfulfilled. The Indians were made wards of the Government and no Indian could testify for himself. After they were stripped of their land they were rounded up and shipped west of the Mississippi River. We cannot but flinch at the ruthlessness of those responsible at the time.

Many times the little arrowhead I carried in my pocketbook caused me to wonder. . . .

Even today it is a beautiful sight to see the few remaining original longleaf pine forests surrounding Thomasville which have fortunately been protected by plantation owners for posterity. The smooth bodies of the trees, almost 100 feet high, standing on ground covered with wiregrass knee-deep and low-bush turkey acorns, all indicate that the land has never been plowed or disturbed by man. One has to see with his own eyes these forests because the sun strikes the colorful bodies of the huge trees at a different angle every hour of the day. With a little imagination it is possible to see many colors—brown, yellow, blue, purple and red. It has always been a mystery how the root system can support these tall trees in a strong wind.

To the trained eye of a forester it appears that a surveyor might have run a straight line through the woods where the species of pines change with the contour or "lay of the land." Longleaf predominates on the well drained high ground and slash and short leaf on the low soil. In these original forests it is not unusual to find a large longleaf with a scar about waist high which the early settlers chipped seeking a straight grain tree easy to split for fence rail, leaving the cross grain ones standing. Most of these old chipped scars have completely healed over with some incasing objects such as blue water-jugs and tools left by workmen 200 years ago.

The age of some of the largest trees is unbelievable. I have a cross section of an original growth longleaf curly pine made into a table by Mr. Paul Sewell, head of the Thomasville Vocational School, which is over 400 years old. The yearly growth rings are so close together it was necessary to use a microscope to count them and learn that the tree was living when America was discovered.

Today we assist nature by using controlled burning when the sap of the trees is almost dormant in the late winter months. While fire, properly used under good supervision, benefits our forests it is true that the rosin in the old heavy scars of the once turpentined trees usually burns some each time until the tree

A rail fence (split with an ax from a straight-grained longleaf pine) such as the ones built by the early settlers.

eventually falls.

From many causes, some natural but more man-made, the original forests are gradually losing their huge trees, older than any living thing around, while all too often we fail to bring about or even encourage the reproduction necessary to take their place. Therefore, the following color pictures were made to

forests which only God could have created.

Pinetree Boulevard circles Thomasville a distance of about two miles from the courthouse and goes through a portion of Greenwood Plantation which contains one of these interesting, historical and beautiful forests. Thousands of people travel this public road to get a view of the grand old forest. Green-

This road leads to Melrose Plantation, originally owned by Paul Coalson and purchased in 1891 by Howard Melville Hanna. It was passed down to his son, Howard Melville Hanna, Jr., and is occupied today by his children, Mrs. Julian C. Bolton and Mrs. Warren Bicknell, Jr.

give future generations some idea of the beauty of these great forests when the Indians roamed them long ago.

No temple ever built by man has been more inspiring than the original longleaf

wood Plantation is owned by J. H. (Jock) Whitney, who was once ambassador to England and is well known in the financial world. He is deeply attached to his plantation and a great friend to the Thomasville area.

Pinetree Boulevard, going through Greenwood Plantation.

When a layman looks at a grand old tree it may be hard for him to believe that its growth is derived solely from the soil and air. The roots collect and feed the tree with water and mineral substances which move upward through channels in the trunk and branches to the leaves. The leaves act as factories where materials necessary for growth are digested and sent to living parts of the tree.

Most trees grow in height and diameter by sending out shoots formed by development of new wood cells. The yearly growth in height is made at the terminal bud while the diameter or thickness grows through additions each year of a layer of new wood cells which are called the annual rings. These rings may be seen on a cross section of the trunk. The wood next to the bark is known as sapwood, because it is living wood which takes up water from the roots and passes it on to the crown. Sapwood eventually changes to heartwood which is darker and lifeless but supports living parts of the tree.

Cells between the last layer of sapwood

A view of the original longleaf forest on Melrose Plantation.

A view of some of the fine old trees on Millpond Plantation.

and the bark make up what is known as cambium layer. Here the new growth takes place. Outside this cambium which forms both wood and bark there is another cambium which makes the corky bark.

All of this is a miracle to man. The heart of an original longleaf pine exposed to the weather lasts longer than any wood grown in our section. This fact was demonstrated to me when I cruised the Whitaker timber and there found an ax that had been buried into a fat lightwood post about the size of a railroad crosstie. I was told that during 1863 the owner of the place was cutting wood with an ax when the Confederate Army sent out to conscript him. He became so mad he buried his ax into the post and there it stayed for 75 years until it rusted out and fell, but the post still remains.

Another section of the magnificent longleaf forest on Greenwood Plantation.

CHAPTER TWO

A study of the arrowheads found here-abouts reveals much about the Indians who inhabited this country before America was discovered. After the white man came along with his different ways and life-style the land-scape and the environment changed drasti-cally—usually for the worse, from a stand-point of natural beauty.

The Indians could not understand personal ownership, why anyone would want to gather unto himself all the land he possibly could and then do with it anything he desired. They themselves did not despoil the land, they were not wasteful hunters and took only that which they could eat. Accordingly, they were our first conservationists. It is estimated that there were between two and three million Indians in the territory now the United States.

The arrowheads, spearheads, dart points and other Indian relics found by those persons who put together the collections shown in this book will serve to give future generations an insight to the early history of the American Continent and especially the Thomasville-Tallahassee-Albany section. There are many great collections in addition to those shown herein, as quite a few persons in the area have made a hobby of hunting arrowheads.

Also, archeologists continue to locate In-dian mounds, campsites and settlements that have long been abandoned and are now grown up in trees to become a part of a forest. After securing permission they unearth these places in search of artifacts which throw still more light on the Indian culture.

Arrowheads are still found in almost every location but more often near the branches and rivers, which indicates this is where the In-dians hunted mostly for their game. Over the long period of time, leaves and accumulated duff have completely covered most of the arrowheads and the best place to look for them is in a freshly plowed plot of "new ground" after a hard rain has exposed the flint by washing away the dirt.

It is interesting to listen to a good collector describe the exact spot where each specimen was found. The excitement of recovering an arrowhead is the rewarding factor, not the actual possession, as many collectors frown upon purchasing them.

The Indians evidently collected flint and other materials in their roamings and then shaped artifacts in different locations. Judging by the large number of artifacts recovered to date and the information of geologists we learn two facts. First, there were many In-dians in this area, and second, they were here for a long, long time. Some of the relics have been dated as far back as 4500 B.C.

At the right is the entrance to Mistletoe Plantation, home of Mr. and Mrs. Gurnee Gallien, located on the Meridian Road at the Georgia-Florida boundary line. The Ochlocknee River flows along the western edge of this large tract of land for a distance of four or five miles, making it a natural habitat for wild game. An Indian mound still remains on the place, although archeologists who examined it found very little of value. Mr. Gallien began searching for arrowheads during 1954 while walking over the plantation after the fields were turned for planting and found the specimens shown below. Many of them are centuries old and were lost by Indians in one of their favorite hunting areas.

Ray Gainey was a small boy living with his father on Mistletoe Plantation when he saw Mr. Gallien's collection of arrowheads. He was inspired to search for many years before discovering and putting together the beautiful collection shown below.

The specimens contain every color in the rainbow and are of many different sizes and shapes. The flint used to make them came from different locations and they were used to shoot all the large and small game found in our area.

Mr. Gainey deserves great credit for recovering these arrowheads. The collection should be preserved for posterity and everyone interested in our history will be grateful for this outstanding contribution.

William D. Cox of Chicago, Illinois, purchased Merryway Plantation from Mr. Nicholas about 1946. This property is south of Thomasville on the Monticello Highway and is bordered on the west by the Old Boston Road.

Mr. Cox continued to increase the acreage of this plantation by making additional purchases and has taken a personal interest in

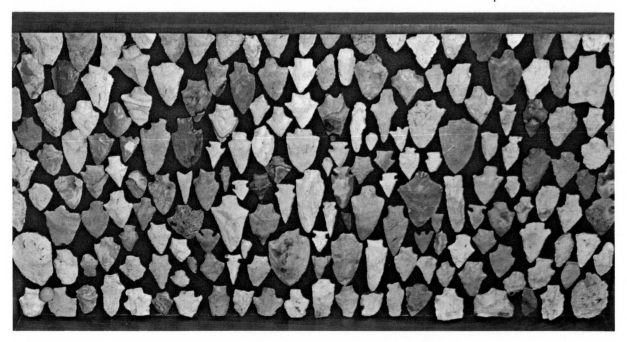

having the brush and worthless hardwood removed with heavy machinery. As the bulldozers disturbed the soil Mr. and Mrs. Cox began discovering arrowheads when they would appear after a hard rain. For fifteen years they have periodically searched and found the remarkable group of Indian arrowheads shown here as "Mr. and Mrs. William D. Cox Collection, Merryway Plantation."

Anyone can imagine the great determina-

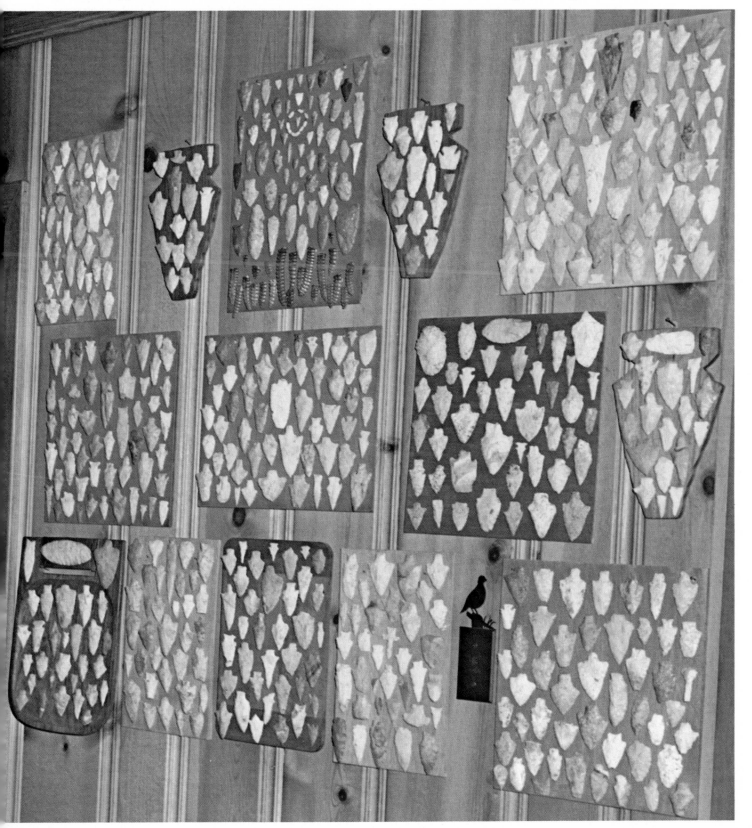

tion and interest it required to accomplish this feat even if the owners enjoyed their effort.

For many years Mr. Cox has entered a dog in the Georgia-Florida Field Trial. The rules of this organization require the owner or trainer to flush the quail and shoot over the dog for the judges to determine if the dog is steady to shot and wing.

As Bill Cox was dismounting to fire a gun over his dog which was on point, his eyes caught a glimpse of a perfect arrowhead and for a second he was torn between taking a chance of the gallery flushing the nervous quail which would have scored against his dog while he retrieved the arrowhead or hurrying to perform his duty. That was one

arrowhead Bill Cox found but didn't add to his collection.

Mr. and Mrs. Cox have many friends in Thomasville and are involved in the welfare of the town, especially the John D. Archbold Memorial Hospital.

They can be located on Rose Show Day sitting with Dr. and Mrs. Fred Murphy in their reserved seats at the Triangle Service Station, always enjoying the spirit of that celebrated day as the three mile parade of floats and bands pass by.

History and Archeology have always interested Bolling Jones, III. When the Scrolls from Qumran in the area of the Dead Sea were found and brought new light to the

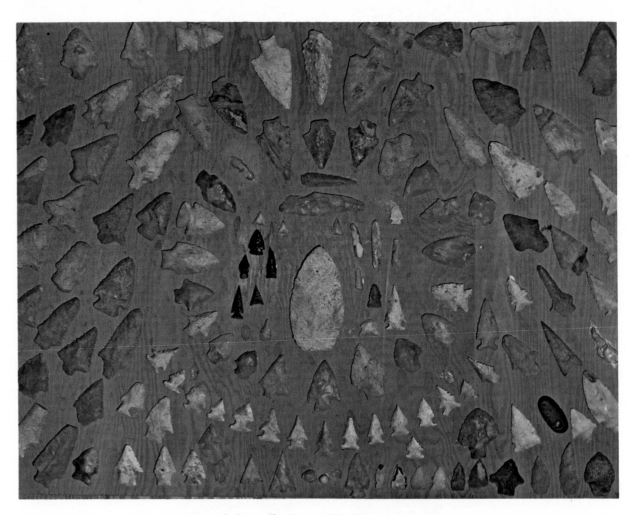

One of the collections of Bolling Jones, III.

16

ancient Scriptures, he did considerable reading on the subject and gave several talks tying the Scrolls into the historical background of the Old and New Testaments.

Bolling has also made a hobby of collecting old weapons, guns, pistols, etc. Distance means very little to him if he wants to investigate a handmade Kentucky rifle or some historical pistol to add to his collection.

When Bolling moved to Thomasville from Atlanta he learned that Myrtlewood Plantation and the Disston Place, owned by Balfour Land Company, contained several old Indian campsites. He began searching for artifacts during his spare moments with good results,

especially near the Ochlocknee River which winds through Myrtlewood a distance of five or six miles. His two sons, Bolling IV and Mike, followed in their father's footsteps and entered into the search, making several collections, one of which is shown here.

When my son, Robert C. Balfour, III, was old enough to accompany me in the woods, it was with great pride that I instructed him how to yelp up a wild turkey or show him the proper way to hold a gun pointed up while approaching a dog pointing a covey of quail, always keeping the safety on until the birds flush and the gun levels on the target.

The memory of companionship is the

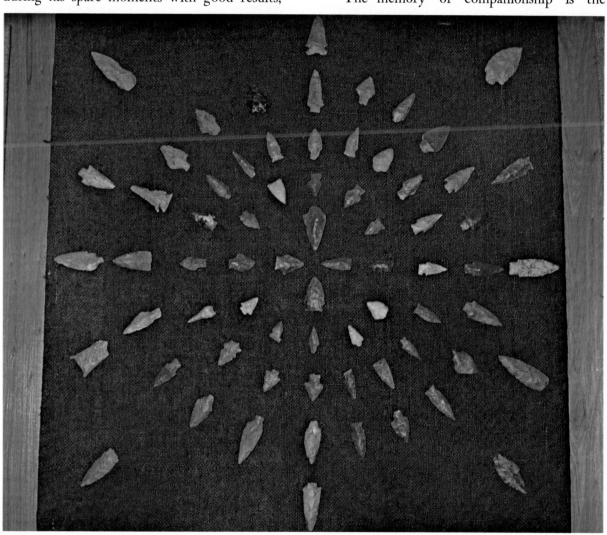

One of the collections of Robert C. Balfour, III.

greatest heritage a father can leave his son. In my case it was a satisfying and refreshing thought to know I was handing down to a succeeding generation the love of the outdoors and the accompanying desire for conservation of our forests and wild game. Every landowner should want to improve the land and leave it in a more productive state than he found it.

Bob is now a practical forester with a working knowledge of trees and agronomy. It was

bany Junior Museum, the first brickhouse built in Albany. This collection is considered one of the finest in the country and a number of years ago the National Geographic Magazine published some of the fine cuts of the outstanding pieces. The accompanying picture will give an idea of the quality of this fine and large collection.

Because of his many years of studying Indian lore as a hobby and his knowledge of where Indian villages were located he served

natural for him, while inspecting a stand of timber, to accidentally find a few arrowheads and he quickly became interested in them.

Many of the arrowheads in his collection shown here were found on the Spring Hill Road when a bulldozer blade uncovered an old Indian Mound while making a new right of way and are of a prehistoric age.

Other collections were found on the Balfour Land Company property, along with a few from Highlands, North Carolina. All of Bob's collections are interesting and have a meaning in the history of our section.

Henry Thomas McIntosh spent forty years collecting artifacts of the Lower Creek Indians, all of them from the Southwest Georgia area. He later presented them to the City of Albany and they are now housed in the Al-

often as a guide to Boy Scout troops and other young people, directing them to the best spots for finding Indian relics.

Henry McIntosh was born in Quitman, Georgia, June 17, 1874, son of Annie White and Henry Martyn McIntosh. His father was the founder of the Quitman Free Press but later moved to Albany where he founded the Albany Herald.

Henry joined his father on the paper in 1892 and served on the staff until his father's death in 1925, at which time he became editor and publisher. He sold the newspaper to James H. Gray in December of 1946.

It was through the courtesy of Henry McIntosh's daughter, Mrs. Martha (George W.) Nall, that much of this information was secured.

CHAPTER THREE

After the hapless Indians were defeated and those remaining were shipped off to reservations the early settlers turned their attention to establishing permanent homes. The cupolas or lookouts on the houses to watch for Indian attacks were being removed while surveyors were busy running lines to determine the best route to build the railroads, among them the short line between Tallahassee and St. Marks.

The short line surveyors hired a young full-blooded Indian helper named Joe Rainwater who had been raised by a white family. Joe had a dark red complexion, stood straight, almost six feet tall, was well coordinated and could ride anything with four legs. He was real quiet and acted as a scout for the surveyors when the going got rough.

Joe had roamed through the Aucilla River Swamp as far north as the spot where the Bellamy Bridge is now located and he was familiar with Sneed's Smoke House, Bennetts Flats, Pine Island, Linton's Lake, the settlements of Aucilla, Lamont, Walker Springs and all the way down the river to Gambol Springs where the river disappears under the ground for a half mile, which location is called Half-Mile-Rise. Nutall-Rise, and the camps at the mouth of the river where it empties into the Gulf were also places known to Joe. He often rode a horse over to the Wacissa River and visited the three big crystal clear springs, Big Blue Springs and two small ones that make up the Wacissa which flows into the Aucilla.

All of this territory was a natural habitat for game and fish 140 years ago and has remained in a wild, unspoiled state. The following pictures show a few of the noted places as they appear today.

The water in Sneed's Smokehouse, a lime sink located near the run of the Aucilla River, drains out through the bottom and refills in the same way.

The Aucilla River, meaning "River of many faces," varies from flat swamps with no distinguishable channel to deep, swift rushing water between steep banks and then disappears in the ground at times for a distance of a half-mile or so. The two scenes shown are quiet lakes through which the Aucilla River passes.

Nutall Rise, the last location where the Aucilla River comes above the ground in its course to the Gulf of Mexico, a distance of six miles. It is very deep at this point and the picture shows one of the many camps.

The canal connecting the Wacissa and Aucilla Rivers was dug by Mr. Nutall with slave labor through the swamps for a mile and a quarter.

Scene after the Wacissa and Aucilla Rivers join.

"Goose Pasture," an area on the Wacissa River picturing the clear water of the river.

Cypress swamp of the Aucilla River changes to solid stand of gum then to high oak hammocks and finally to pure cabbage palm near the Gulf of Mexico.

This shows one of the many small rises where the Aucilla River reappears from underground. The reflection of the trees on the water provokes a close study to take in the beauty of this rare scene.

Hammock type swamp showing mixed stand of cabbage palm and pine in the Aucilla River Swamp.

Scene showing entry into the Aucilla River Swamp with modern road.

One of many hunting camps in the Aucilla Swamp. Local hunters spend up to two weeks living in this type camp during deer season. Some of the camps are reached only by boat.

Even though Joe Rainwater was reared in the home of a white family with their own children, apart from all other Indians, and had the opportunity to learn to read and write, he never forgot his own people. He clearly remembered when his mother and father were taken away with the rest of the tribe from the land they loved and called their own.

All the land down the Aucilla River and the country between Thomasville and Tallahassee teemed with wild game and by the time Joe was grown he was a skilled hunter and woodsman.

The security of a home with the family that raised him was not sufficient to keep Joe from becoming lonesome for companionship because there were no Indian girls around. The white girls looked down on him while the black girls were afraid. It was therefore natural to seek the woods and be with the wild creatures with whom he felt a bond. Just to sit on the high bluff of a deep clear spring in the shade of the moss covered oak trees and pitch a pebble into the water and see a bass swim up to investigate the sudden splash instinctively brought Joe pleasure. Or, to witness the bravery of a wild turkey hen caring for her brood in the spring of the year as she chased down a large grasshopper, divided it with her chicks and a moment later teamed up with a big gobbler to fight off a rattlesnake threatening her young.

Joe had the born instinct to sit motionless in the forest and watch the wild creatures feed and move around in their natural habitat. Only one like Joe, who was a part of the woods, would have noticed a pair of small birds no larger than a man's thumb strip the lichen from the bark of a tree and securely fasten a tiny nest to a swinging branch entirely out of the reach of a predator. He knew the birds had never been instructed about how to build a nest. Neither had they ever witnessed one in the making. Yet with their feet and bill every dry twig, blade of grass and even snake egg casings were placed in the exact right spot to form a perfect nest in which to lay their eggs.

Joe would watch motionlessly when he saw a large hawk dive on a snake with lightning speed and striking force enough to wound or kill the dangerous reptile, then fly away with the prey firmly held in its talons.

All the sights and the sounds of the forest were familiar to him—a squirrel caught in the claws of a large owl, begging for mercy, the plea of a bullfrog being swallowed by a water moccasin, the squeal of a rabbit caught by a wildcat, the distress sound of a quail caught in the air by a Blue Darter hawk, the joyful song of birds during the nesting season or the contented honk of geese starting back to Canada after a hard winter in the South. The interpretation and meaning of all was as difficult as a scholar learning ten foreign languages.

Watching the freedom of the wild life, the antics of the 'coons, oppossums and once in a while a black bear or deer seemed to bring peace into Joe's heart. He would often stretch out on the ground and gaze up at the blue sky, content in the knowledge that the woods was his home with all of God's creatures.

Long after the railroad to St. Marks was completed Joe met a tenant farmer's daughter who was not afraid of him because he was an Indian and they were married.

About fifty years after Joe Rainwater was married I got to know a guide on Lake Iamonia by the name of Majo Mical who was half Indian. His coarse black hair, coppery complexion, quiet disposition and graceful, fluid movements whether he was pushing a boat or stalking game all confirmed his Indian ancestry. Majo had the know-how to place a hunter in a position on the Lake to bag more wild ducks or catch more fish than any guide on the Lake and was much in demand.

There were sometimes long moments on a duck hunt when you could not see a duck or hear a gun fire and Majo sat in the boat scanning the skies, still as a stone statue. During one of these quiet periods I asked Majo if he remembered his father. After a long silence he replied, "Yes." Realizing I could not push him, I asked how old he was when his father died and he said, "About fourteen." "What was his name?" He replied, "Joe Rainwater. He worked on the railroad between Tallahassee and St. Marks." "Why are you named Majo Mical?" "That's always been my name," was his reply.

Gradually, Majo revealed that his father had left the railroad and wandered around working at many different places until he found a small tenant house on a farm near Lake Iamonia. There he had the freedom to hunt and fish on this large body of water which belonged to the State of Florida and he was happy. Majo was nurtured and brought up on the fish and game his father got from Lake Iamonia and in that environment his natural talent was developed from early childhood.

How lucky and happy I was to have him

for my trusted guide, companion and friend! He understood the habits of wild game and always disregarded his comfort and welfare for my success and pleasure. Even the silent moments we spent together waiting for ducks to fly or fish to bite brought about an understanding and developed a confidence we seemed to possess in each other that became almost sacred.

Sitting in a boat with a guide who only expressed himself by the sound of a grunt or once in a while saying yes or no could easily become tiresome. But after Majo developed complete confidence in me and felt at ease there were many moments of great interest and enjoyment.

"Were you real young when your 'Father Joe' started taking you into the woods hunting?" I once asked.

"Yes," he replied, "I remember my first trip with him. He taught me how to walk in the dry leaves inches deep on the ground without making a noise when he was hunting squirrels one afternoon in the Aucilla Swamp. After bagging two squirrels a heavy fog settled over the area causing darkness to descend upon us. This would have scared me to death, but father was at home in the woods and did not give me time to worry. He realized we could not find our way out without the guidance of the sun or stars and began preparing to spend the night. With only his pocketknife he cut the framing for a shelter from the stems of hardwood brush, used forked uprights and tied them together with poles and braces. He selected the mound of a blown-down tree to build the hut against and covered it with palmetto palms by platting the long stems together. After stripping the moss from nearby trees to make a mattress he started a fire to cook the squirrels. It was only then that I realized my fright was gone and I was enjoying a wonderful experience with my father.

"About first dark the deep bass voice of bullfrogs from a nearby lagoon caused father to sharpen a long buttonwood spear, give me a lightwood torch to hold high above my head and say, 'Come on, let's get some froglegs for breakfast.' How exciting it was to see the red eyes of these game creatures at night and know your success depended on steady nerves. We managed to get plenty for breakfast."

It rained all night as Majo wrapped up in the moss and slept while his father caught short naps, kept the fire going and watched for the vicious wild boars that ranged through the swamp.

Majo said he dreamed about a long black bug that flew around in the daylight because it couldn't see at night. It spent the night in a dark stall in the mountainside. Suddenly it was awakened by a wonderful soft light and looked down and saw a young beautiful woman with a baby in her arms and all about was the beautiful light. Then an angel came into the stall and as the little bug was looking on with excitement the angel took a green jewel from her crown and laid it down on the black bug. The bug said, "Ouch!", but the angel only arranged her crown, picked up the jewel, put it back into place and vanished. It was then the bug realized that the back part of his body was lighted up with the color of the jewel and that he had been present when our Lord Jesus Christ was born. Thus lightning bugs by the millions are today carrying the light of Christ to all the dark spots of the world.

I did not tell Majo that his dream was a portion of an old legend handed down for generations. Instead, I inquired if he and his father had had any trouble getting out of the Aucilla Swamp that next morning.

Majo said, "We ate a breakfast of roasted froglegs and started walking in the opposite direction of the sun and eventually came upon a large opening in the swamp which father called a prairie. The outline of trees on the opposite side of the prairie was barely visible and the entire areas seemed to be covered with coarse grass about knee-high with several round cypress islands appearing every now and then. The ground was spongy peat moss and soft black muck, occasionally interspersed with solid soil."

There is a supposition that water in the Aucilla Slough is purified as it filters through these prairie spots and joins the river further downstream. In dry periods the peat moss often burns for months causing large holes to appear, but in rainy spells these cavities fill again.

The calm disposition of Majo changed to one of excitement when he described the sights and hazards they encountered while crossing the prairie. First, the skeletons of several cows that had ventured out too far to graze and had become bogged up in the black muck. Then witnessing several droves of Canadian Geese light in freshly burned spots and feed on the tender sprouts of vegetation. The difficulty of crawling through the maiden reeds dragging a shotgun, afraid they would come upon a cottonmouth moccasin any time. And finally, watching his father kill a ten pound gander and wound another which they retrieved.

Just before they reached the woodsline someone shot a rifle in their direction and Father Joe stopped and turned towards the left. He told the boy it was a swamper making "licker" and he had shot to warn them to stay away.

Never would Majo have told this story unless he felt at ease with me, and I considered it a compliment.

Lake Iamonia, located in Florida near the Georgia border line, covers approximately 5,000 acres. A subterranean passage, called the sink, drained the lake periodically in very long dry spells. Sometimes the water would stay in the lake for twenty years and in other periods it would go dry every five or six years. This condition existed until a dam was constructed to hold the water in the main body of the lake so it could not drain or run out through the underground passage, thereby eliminating the long periods when the lake would be dry. It was claimed that the water came back into the lake in ex-

ceedingly rainy periods through the same subterranean passage it went out. To prove this, large fish could be caught a few weeks after the water returned. The Ochlocknee River and many other streams dump great quantities of water into the lake during flood stages.

Lake Iamonia is covered with lily pads and coontail moss except for about 200 acres in the basin and strand. Alligators make many clear water holes among the bonnets by rooting out the vegetation and pushing it to one side. Over a long period this debris forms a tussock. The male alligator is often seen lying on a tussock—sleeping, sunning or, during the mating season, bellowing mightily for such an unromantic-looking creature. If they are with young, both "gator" parents become aggressive and dangerous.

At one time alligators were very numerous and the older fishermen swear the more gators in the lake the better the fishing. Alligators often crawl long distances through the swamp or woods going from one body of water to the other.

In the early thirties it was quite an occasion when the new model automobiles were unveiled. Bill MacIntyre and Jack Turner were Ford agents in Thomasville. Bill and a friend were driving the first new model of the year back from Jacksonville and in every town they passed through, crowds of people made a quick inspection.

Just before dark they noticed an alligator about three feet long crossing the road. They caught it and put it in the back of the new car, then forgot about it when they stopped for a bite to eat. When they came out of the restaurant a large crowd surrounded the new Ford, standing back a respectful distance. Bill was delighted and invited the viewers to go on up and inspect the car closer. But they only stepped back, explaining that one of them had opened the back door and jumped in to "try it for size." It was dark, and only a split second later the

Billy Cochran (formerly Boree Club) built by
Clayton Lindsay, Kent Sanders, Sam Alexander and H. H. Callahan, Thomasville, Fla.
der and H. H. Callahan, Thomasville, Ga.

Billy Cochran (E. A. (Rob) Robinson Camp)
Thomasville, Ga.

Steyerman Camp (built by Leb Dekle and Steyerman Bros.) Now owned by Joe Walthall-
Real Estate

W. C. Johnson, Thomasville, Ga.

James Crosby, Thomasville, Ga.

Don Singletary, Thomasville, Ga.

Russell Dickey, (house across street owned by
Anna Bell Sloan) Thomasville, Ga.

Carlton Steward, Thomasville, Ga. (house across
street owned by Allen Baggett, Cairo, Ga.)

J. C. Hendricks, Thomasville, Ga. (trailer across
street owned by R. N. Johnson, Elkhart, Ind.)

Yuvawn Willis, Maurice Willis, Leslie Barrett,
Sonny Marshall, Cairo, Ga.

Jimmy Hart, Thomasville, Ga.

Jimmy Hendricks, Thomasville, Ga.

Bud Vereen, Moultrie, Ga.

J. V. Smith, Tallahassee, Fla.

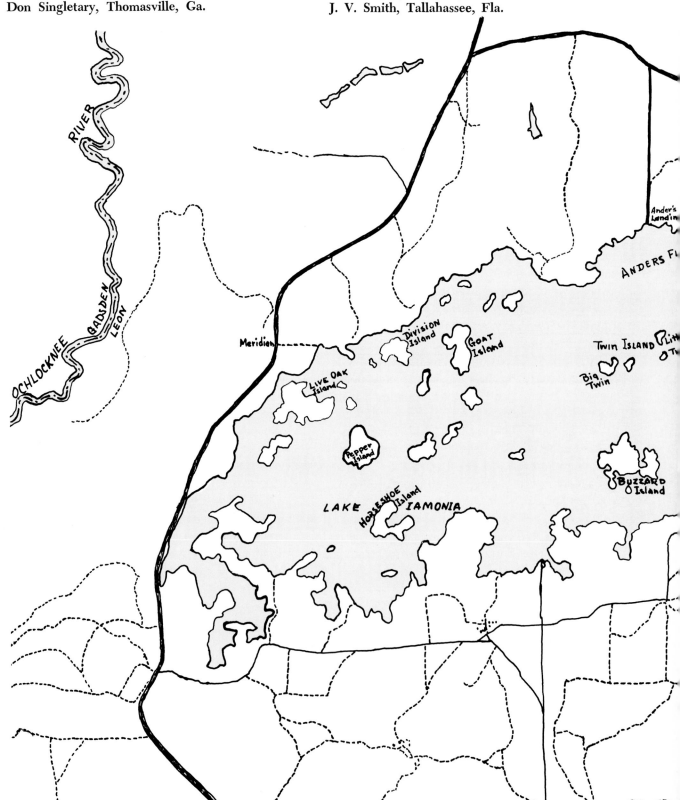

North Shore of Lake Iamonia

A. R. Beverly, Tallahassee, Fla.

Aubrey Barrow, Tallahassee, Fla.

Mallory Horne, Tallahassee, Fla.

Frank Pidcock, Moultrie, Ga.

Bullneck Lodge (Cochran Scott, Jimmy Keyton, C. W. McKinnon, Jr., Tommy Dixon) formerly Dixon Camp

T. W. White, Cairo, Ga.

Iamonia Gun Club (Forrest Knapp, Jr., Osborne Chastain, Jack Crawford, Victor Beadles, Howard Cheshire, Dewey Reaves, Lonnie Pope and Warren Taylor)

Sam Pierce, Cairo, Ga.

Sunnyland Camp, Thomasville, Ga.

Duck Haven Gun Club—Jimmy Anderson, Chris Cocroft, Harry Jones, Langdon Flowers, W. H. Flowers, Roscoe Fleetwood, Ralph Faulk, Dan Kelly, Buddy Hines, Ed Frechtling, Nat Williams, Tommy Howkins, Bill Watt, Robert Jinright, Bryan Robinson, William McCollum, Heyward Vann, George Lane, Dick Singletary, Heeth Varnedoe, III

Murray Maxwell, Cairo, Ga.

L. W. Seabrook, Tallahassee, Fla.

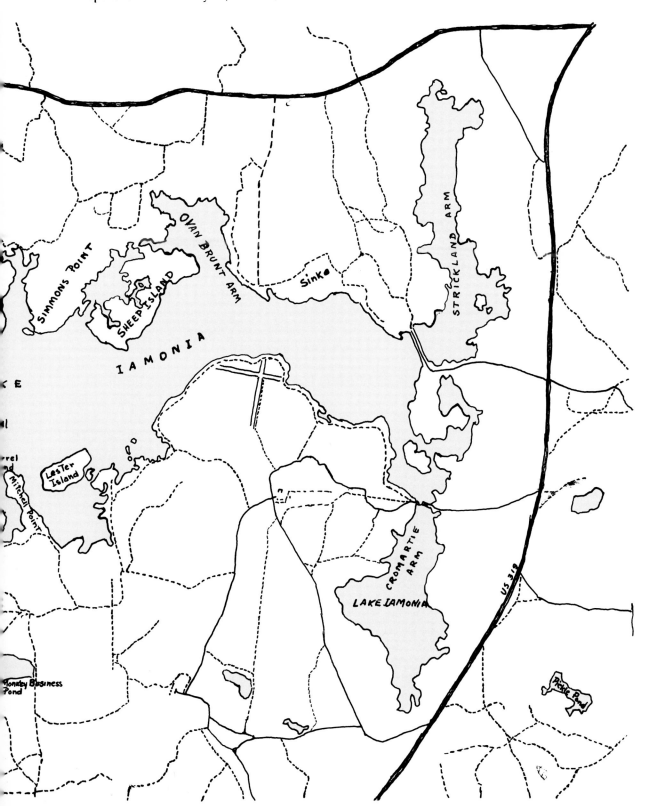

man, ashen with terror, shot out of the car as if from a catapult. After his friends ran him down and caught him he swore he had been attacked in the car by a rattlesnake the size of his leg.

In recent years air boats have illegally been used on Lake Iamonia to slaughter thousands of alligators for their skins.

This map gives in detail a complete picture of Lake Iamonia. It shows the points of interest, the boat landings and location of private hunting camps. There is no record available which gives the names of the islands in the lake. Only by talking to old residents and boatmen who spent their lives on Iamonia was it possible to secure the names used.

Majo Mical became more than a guide—he was a sincere friend. Before day one morning I was in the front of his sharp pointed boat with my gun and decoys while he stood in the back pushing us smoothly over the lilly pads with a reed pole about eight feet long. It takes an expert to locate a duck blind before daylight on a freezing morning. There were no markers or guide-posts—we knew only the general direction we should take. Neither of us was talking, just wondering where our duck blind was, when suddenly Majo's pole went into a gator hole as he leaned on it. There was no bottom and over he went, head-over-heels into the water. He made a few splashes and pulled himself back into the boat, never saying a word. Long after our decoys were out and we were in the blind, Majo said, "You know what? I always made up my mind if I ever fell into a gator hole dat gator had to swallow me crossways 'cause I wasn't about to go straight down."

Lake Iamonia grows more natural wild duck food than any lake in our section and I have shot ducks on it for fifty years. In normal times the lake is five or six feet deep in the areas where the ducks feed and it is difficult to construct a blind. Usually a hunter drives four long posts into the mud and nails strips about 1″ by 2″ to hold them

in position. Then myrtle bushes, dog fennel or leafy branches are placed along the strips. This kind of blind keeps the boat steady when the hunter stands to shoot and also conceals him from a flight of ducks.

One rule of the lake is nearly always re-spected. The man who builds a blind has first claim on it only for the opening day of the duck season. In the balance of the season the hunter who gets there first has the right to use it. Some hunters have built gates at one end and locked them and others have burned a lantern inside the blind all night.

The hardships a hunter endures and the terrific expense he stands to kill a duck is unbelievable to a non-hunting, or "normal," man. However, to a sportsman who has seen a hundred Ringneck ducks fall out of the skies with their necks stretched, aiming straight for his decoys and sounding like a roaring express train traveling one hundred miles an hour, costs and hardships are com-pletely inconsequential.

One morning Majo pushed our boat into a duck blind long before day. Everything was still as we sat watching a glow appear in the east even though it stayed dark on the lake. I finally said, "Majo, you know what I am thinking?", but Majo didn't answer me for we were both thinking at that moment about God's creation and how great God was. The ducks were leaving the lake, we could hear the wings of thousands of them overhead but there wasn't enough light to distinguish any movement and we remained crouched in the little duck boat straining our eyes. Eventually old Majo said, "I can just 'zern' 'em! Shoot straight up overhead—there are so many you can't miss." I shot at the next noisy swish of wings and a duck fell with a loud splash.

Aware of the lucky shot, we continued to strain our eyes hoping the visibility would soon improve. Majo finally said, "Ducks feed all night in bright moonlight," and we began to relax as the noise of flapping wings faded from the air. The freezing weather had forced the ducks south and there were many Ringnecks (usually called "Bullnecks"), Widgeons, Pintails, Bluebills, Teal, Greenheads and Black Mallards on the lake so we were curious to learn which of these species we had shot.

When daylight came we saw a big Greenhead Mallard drake on the water. Majo pushed the boat out of the blind and retrieved the handsome duck. On the duck's leg we found a band which read, "Write Box 48, Kingsville, Ont." On the inside of the band was a verse of Scripture, "He careth for you. I Pet. 5:7." I wrote to this address, describing Lake Iamonia and the date I shot the Mallard and got a fine reply from a man named Jack Miner who later sent me his book.

Jack Miner was a great hunter and during his early life shot for the market, but he soon decided that this kind of shooting was, as he said, "murder in the first degree," and he started hunting only for pleasure and for food. In 1902 he secured some wild duck eggs and raised two hens and a drake. He made an artificial pond and continued raising a few Mallards but kept their wings clipped, or pinioned. By 1908 he decided it was more fun to see them fly around and that fall a bunch of them went away. These same ducks returned the following summer with their young about half grown.

From this little start Jack Miner fed ducks and geese every year and literally thousands of them became his pets before they migrated south for the winter.

From a Salvation Army lassie he bought a calendar that had a verse from the Bible for every day in the year. He selected several of the verses, such as "From this day I will bless you," and stamped them on the inside of an aluminum band. He wrote, "In less than a week I had the fowls of the air carrying the Word of God, and in six months they were delivering it from the sunny side of the Atlantic to the far off Indians and Esqumaux of the Hudson Bay."

It is hard to believe that wild ducks and geese on Jack Miner's lake became so tame they would eat out of his hand. For these same birds to migrate south for the open shooting season, have hunters constantly taking pot shots at them, then so many of the survivors return to Jack Miner and immediately show no fear is little short of phenomenal.

When I told Majo what Jack Miner was doing for the ducks he grunted, "Huh! Good —good, that's good."

"Well, Majo," I said, "you are going to become famous because Jack Miner has written in his book about the Mallard we killed and our names are mentioned."

If Majo was impressed he showed no sign of it. After a long wait he asked, "What did you do with that big duck?"

Not being quite as stoic as Majo, I chuckled heartily. I said I had hung the Mallard, along with fifteen Bullnecks, in the cold storage room at the ice plant. The next morning I went to the ice plant with Ed Jerger, editor of the local newspaper, who was entertaining the Board of Regents of the University System of Georgia, of which he was a member, and who wanted wild ducks for his menu.

When the bunch of ducks which was tied together with a strong cord was placed on the platform and the cord cut, one of the Bullnecks came to and in the ensuing commotion it flew away. Mr. Jerger gave the story to the Associated Press and it was flashed all over America. The members of the Board had a feast on our banded Mallard.

Late in the game season that winter the ducks had thinned out on Lake Iamonia so Majo and I drove over to Lake Jackson and located Pete Rawlings, a boatman who was born and raised on the banks of the lake. He told us there were thousands of ducks rafted up in the Sugar Hole, but the water was much too deep for building a blind. Majo and I set out in a boat for the Hole and we scared up enough ducks to blacken the skies.

I couldn't get those ducks off my mind and finally made a portable blind out of wire and grass. Majo took my decoys out and placed them and I pushed another boat out and chained it to a long pole driven into the mud. I hid the boat with my portable blind and I stretched out in the bottom on my back. Majo said, when he left, "You look like a floating tussock." Evidently the ducks thought so too because they almost knocked me out of the boat, but it was necessary for me to be something of an acrobat and to know how to handle a gun. A confirmed duck hunter will go through almost any hardship for such excitement as I experienced.

When Majo pushed out to pick up the ducks and decoys and saw how successful our portable blind had worked, his face lighted up with satisfaction. This was the first time a hunter had ever bagged the limit of ducks in the deep open "Sugar Hole."

Lake Jackson is one place a man can bag the limit of ducks and catch a good string of bass with a rod and reel while his guide paddles the boat back to the landing. Broadus Willingham, my lifelong friend and shooting partner, and Julian Lewis, both of Macon, Georgia, witnessed one of these occasions.

Every sportsman familiar with Lake Jackson was acquainted with Pete Rawlings, the guide who made his living fishing and hunting. He was a big, strong, exceedingly accommodating black man with a grand deep bass voice which carried over the water for a long distance. His family consisted of a wife and fourteen children. One afternoon I wanted him to fish with me but he was on the lake almost out of sight so I sounded my horn and could distinctly hear him answer in a low normal voice, "I'm coming." After ten minutes elapsed it was possible to recognize Pete, but I could not understand why his fishing boat was flying a flag which would rise ten or twelve feet in the air then settle in the boat and rise again. Even-

tually it was plain to see it was a sea gull which had swallowed his fishbait—Pete was mad at the bird and released it only just before he got to the landing. Pete always left the lake before dark and rang a big bell which notified his children to gather so he could check them, because he lived in dread of an alligator swallowing one of the small ones.

After the wild ducks migrate to their breeding grounds in Canada, people start fishing in the large lakes. While the fishing is nearly always good to excellent, more often than not it is an added event, some unexpected incident, that makes for a really memorable occasion. I remember sitting on the front seat of a small boat threading a flyrod with a Royal Coachman to cast for bream while Majo pushed our boat towards Ander's Flat in the back of Lake Iamonia. It was early in the afternoon and as we neared Duck Haven Camp a soft wind from the Gulf of Mexico brought the sweet scent of magnolia blossoms across the water. I remarked, "Gee, it would be great to see Ander's Hammock while the magnolias are in bloom." Majo did not reply but headed his boat straight for the hammock.

After beaching the boat we walked out into the shaded forest and there we saw magnolia trees fifty feet high with long smooth trunks, probably 200 years old. The tops of the trees almost touched each other and had large green leaves the size of my hand with huge, handsome white blossoms showing through the openings. Last year's leaves had fallen with the cup side up and looked like a beautiful carpet spread on the ground for us to walk on. The deep shade of the trees had smothered the underbrush so it was possible to see a great distance.

The farther we walked the more beautiful and interesting the scene became. That was in June of 1940. The pictures shown were made in June of 1971. This spot is still one of the most beautiful natural wild places in our section. But is so far off the beaten trails

Magnolia trees in Ander's Hammock, bordering Lake Iamonia.

that very few persons have had the pleasure of seeing it.

When we returned to our boat Majo realized our fishing trip had been delayed and glided the boat over the water and bonnets in double quick time. He soon brought it to a sudden stop in the middle of the Flat. Majo placed his pushpole length ways of the boat, picked up the paddle and quietly sat on the back seat letting the boat drift while he watched me cast the little dry-fly. Every now and then the small Royal Coachman would float through the air and light so naturally a redbreast bream, "as big as both a man's hands put together," would strike, find it had been hooked, then stand on its tail and dance over the water and lily pads a distance of five or six feet trying to release the hook. During this excitement I always yelled, "Hold that fish," but Majo never changed expression. When the fish had been landed and placed in the live box a glance at Majo made me feel as if I had been talking to myself.

The bonnets or lily pads in the water of Lake Iamonia make fishing extremely difficult and only those fishermen with experience, patience and know-how are apt to succeed. The thrill of landing the redbreast bream, which feed largely on fresh water shrimp and often weigh over two pounds, is the reward for which the fisherman works so hard.

Another time we were out on the lake late in the afternoon. The sun had disappeared and the next few minutes would be the finest time of the day to make a fish rise to a fly, so I was striving to make every cast a good one. My concentration on letting the dry-fly hit the small clear openings before the line fell on the water seemed to have entranced me completely, because Majo touched me with his boat paddle and pointed to the left where a deer was swimming toward Buzzards Island, a distance of half a mile.

I used the paddle and Majo the push pole

and within a few minutes we pulled up alongside the deer. It looked like an old buck that had shed its antlers and they were returning in velvet. But on further examination we were certain it was a young spiked buck. I had a crazy idea to catch the deer and rope it as a cowboy would a calf by tying its feet together with some 120 pound fishing line.

I leaned over the side of the boat and seized the buck's long ears but they were so slick I could not hold them. I tried again, thinking surely I ought to be able to handle him. But on my third attempt the buck rolled completely over in the water and his hooves came up slashing at my bare arms like a sharp-bladed buzz saw. Before I could realize the danger and get out of the way the blood was trickling down both elbows from the deer's greatest weapon—his razor sharp hooves. The cuts were not deep or serious, and I learned the hard way that a deer is not exactly an ideal wrestling opponent.

Two weeks after we saw the deer in the middle of the lake the urge to cast a fly in Ander's Flat prompted me to drive to Majo's little cabin and pick him up for an afternoon's fishing. When I arrived the shutters on the house were tightly drawn and no sign of life could be detected.

Where was the hound dog that always greeted me? The chickens that roamed the yard? The pig Majo fattened in the pen? I felt lonesome and became uneasy and with my heart pounding I raced to the nearest neighbor a mile away. There I was informed that Majo had died in his sleep a week ago, and his wife had returned to her family.

I lost all desire to fish and started for home, rebuking myself because I had not somehow learned of Majo's death. If I had known I could have at least shown my deep friendship and sympathy for my faithful guide.

For fifteen years I had had a companion who taught me much about the outdoors and wildlife, and this was the end. I became very sad. He never asked for a favor, not even a small one, and was willing to hunt with me when the lake was frozen over or fish when the sun burned through our shirts. His life was typical of his people who only wanted the opportunity to live and be left alone. It is a sad fact that so many of the few Indians who were left in our midst have been entirely swallowed up by our civilization. Majo was the last one I had the privilege of knowing in the Thomasville, Tallahassee and Albany area.

After Majo's death I realized his quiet, patient disposition had taught me how to relax and enjoy a hunting trip. He made me conscious that it was not necessary to carry on a conversation because we could learn more by observing everything around us.

When the ducks were not flying Majo sat in the back of the small boat as silent as a statue except when I became restless and asked a question, and then he usually only grunted.

I would sometimes wonder if Majo was sleeping because there was no communication between us and finally he would arise, pick up the decoys and push our boat to the landing. Before I left, he would explain that the feeding period was over and the weather fixing to change, so he came in. He instinctively knew what to do with game and he would be summarizing the situation when I thought he was asleep.

I know God created the earth and has dominion over it, but it was largely Majo who inspired me to feel God's presence when amongst the trees or on the water in the outdoors. Maybe I still hear Majo whispering, "Do not desecrate this beautiful earth for it is not yours, it belongs to God."

Typical view of Lake Iamonia.

CHAPTER FOUR

Lake Miccosukee is located twelve miles east of Lake Iamonia just south of the Georgia-Florida line and is one of the great natural duck lakes in our section. It is covered with lily pads or bonnets in the deep water and tall grass in the shallow places. After the frost in the fall this grass turns brown. The basin and strand is so deep no vegetation can survive. The area of the lake is several thousand acres and the ducks feed on the seed in the coontail moss and other grasses. After a hunter locates the ducks feeding, drops a few decoys, pushes the sharp-pointed boat into the long dead grass, and stands a few dogfennels along the sides, he is ready to start shooting.

About 1920 there were a good many boatmen, who lived near Lake Miccosukee, ready and willing to carry a hunter or fisherman out in their small boats for very modest fees. These men were characters who spent their entire lives on the lake and had a language all their own. They would guide anyone but preferred to go out with a good shot or a keen fisherman and did not hesitate to brag about those they considered particularly expert.

Tat Brooks favored Albert, Bob and Sid Stringer, three great shots and fine sportsmen. Kirksey was loyal to Dr. John Cone, Allie Robinson and all his family. Van Higdon always worked for Homer Williams,

Temas Drayton for Tom Mardre and John Mitchell seemed to enjoy working for me. All these guides were skillful hunters and all had a strong sporting streak in their make-up.

Nearly all the guides on the lakes were black men who owned small, often rickety boats which contained a live box for the fish. However, during the duck season almost every hunter furnished his guide with a good boat.

Charles Footman and Ben Ford, who stayed near Hopkins Landing on Lake Miccosukee, were excellent boatmen and were familiar with every square foot of the lake. It was these two men who once before daylight heard a voice on the lake calling in a low frightened voice, "On the bottom, on the bottom," and they hurried their boat over and rescued Garry Wade who was standing on the bottom of the lake with his head barely out of the water after his boat had capsized. Garry was the son of J. H. Wade, owner of Mill Pond Plantation, and one of the most beloved of all the area's winter residents. He was an excellent shot, extremely modest, and above all a great friend of mine and of every citizen of Thomasville.

George Morrison was an old guide and fisherman who liked to anchor his boat on the edge of the strand and rig up six fishing poles. He would set the poles in a semicircle and look from one cork to the other all day. He didn't have a worry in the world, but he always did have a live box full of good fish.

May's Pond is only a short distance from Lake Miccosukee—in fact, there is a wet weather drain which connects the two. When Homer Williams and I owned this pond during 1921, thousands of egrets nested and roosted in the trees which grew in the water. The long beautiful plumes of these birds were used to decorate women's hats of that period. Late in the afternoon the egrets came into the pond by the thousands and we often took selected groups to witness the spectacular sight of long strings of these birds gliding from a great height into the trees some distance out in the pond where the varmints couldn't bother them.

During the season a favorite flight pattern of the ducks was between May's Pond and Lake Miccosukee. Late in the afternoon three or four hunters with choked guns would often stand some distance apart on the flyway. When a duck was shot down it usually fell in a cornfield and was retrieved by a bird dog. Just before dark one afternoon a sawbill duck was winged. The retriever ran it down and was in the act of grabbing it when the duck nipped him sharply on the nose. This was the undoing of one of the finest retrievers in the country. He refused from that occasion on to pick up anything with feathers. It was interesting to watch that dog point a dead quail, or, if it was winged and running, slap it with his paw, but he always kept his nose well out of the way.

May's Pond Plantation was later acquired by Capt. H. A. White and is now the property of Mrs. Ralph Perkins.

Lake Iamonia, Lake Miccosukee and Lake Jackson have always been open to the public for those with a hunting and fishing license. They are supervised by State and Federal Game Wardens to enforce the game commission's regulations.

Thousands of outdoorsmen have enjoyed shooting and fishing on these lakes. Some of the best shots in America, visiting the Lakes for the first time, have been embarrassed trying to hit a Bullneck falling out of the clouds at the rate of 150 miles an hour to dive over the decoys. The experienced hunter usually waits to shoot until the ducks slow down and make their second effort to decoy.

For many years range cattle grazed the land adjoining the western end of Lake Iamonia. When the grass became scarce the cows waded out into the lake to eat the water plants and would go from one island to the other in search of food. The constant use of these cow trails killed the vegetation and the bottom became filled with white sand, covered by the dark clear water. Sometimes during the rainy season it became necessary for the cows to swim in the deepest part of the trails.

During the full moon in April, May and June the bass all over the lake spawned in the white sand of these cow trails, with their tails fanning out a round saucer shaped place about two feet in diameter and then depositing their eggs.

Sam Jones lived with his wife and many small children within a few feet of Lake Iamonia and was the caretaker of Duck Haven Camp. An excellent boatman, he habitually kept me posted as to the time the bass were on the beds.

One year during the full moon in May, Sam placed me in the front of his boat and quietly let his boat move down the cow trails. I was casting with an old rod and reel and using a lure called a "crippled minnow." We waited until a "bed-minder" chased the minnows away, which was a sure sign that a big bass was on its bed or nearby. At that moment I would cast my lure over the spot and with a short motion of the wrist try to attract the bass, all the while keeping braced for a fight with an eight or ten pounder.

To land the limit of huge bass in one

afternoon was an experience not soon forgotten. Of course, there were also days when we fished the cow trails and waited for a bed-minder to break the water without seeing a ripple or getting a nibble.

Sitting quietly in a boat and waiting for fish to feed could become boring, but not with Sam Jones. On one occasion I asked Sam how he made a living for his large family and he said, "I fishes and preach."

"What kind of preacher are you?" I asked.

"Just a stump knocker," he replied.

Not sure what he meant, I tried another tack. "Well, what do you preach about?"

After taking a deep breath Sam grinned and said, "I just reads a verse in the Bible and proceeds to coordinate it with the congregation."

I liked that so much I asked him again what he had said and he simplified his answer by stating, "I reads a verse in the Bible and proceeds to atomize it."

Sam's simple life—fishing, hunting and preaching—never became humdrum to him or anyone around. His deep bass voice was known by all the boatmen on the lake and he could converse with very little effort to other boatmen a half mile away. He would call in a low vibrating voice, "Andrew—George, you got any fish?" He was so far away a little time elapsed before the answer came back, "Yeah, you want 'em?"

Sam's voice over the water sounded like a tuba in a symphony orchestra and it prompted me to remark, "Gee, with your voice you should make your church members sit up and take notice."

He said, "Yes sir, I does."

"How do you go about arousing them, Sam?"

"Well, I gets up and tells 'em, then I tells 'em what I told 'em, and by the time I am through telling 'em they all knows the facts."

Duck Haven Club camp is at the edge of Lake Iamonia and faces Andrew's Flat. It was organized by Staley and Worth Upchurch, two prominent business men and fine

marksmen of Thomasville, and the land purchased from Judge Andrews.

Staley and Worth would handle a boat as well as any guide. One freezing morning before daylight they pushed out to their duck blind and were throwing out their decoys when Staley in his haste tangled the string of a decoy around Worth's gun and threw it in the lake. There were a great many ducks on the lake and Worth had to have his gun. Without hesitation he stripped off his clothes dived overboard and was in the act of retrieving it when a guest from one of the Northern owned plantations heard and saw the commotion in the water and naturally assumed someone was in dire need of help. With his guide helping he quickly paddled over and said, "Is there anything I can assist with?"

Worth came up out of the water, dropped his gun over the side of the boat, pulled up on the back seat, naked as a jay bird except for the streamers of coontail moss still on his head and said, "No sir, thank you, I am out to kill a brace of ducks and always take a dip in the lake before I start shooting—it settles my nerves."

The startled guest took one look and sputtered to his guide, "Let's get away from here." And as the visitor's boat faded in the morning mist Worth heard him say, "Those people are crazy!"

When the large redbreast bream are on the beds many fishermen hunt the lake trying to locate them. On a bed that hasn't been fished one can make a fine catch, but its impossible to keep it a secret and other boats soon crowd in and spoil the fun.

Sam Jones always took me away from the basin end of the lake and we probed around where very few fishermen ever went, spending a great deal of time hunting bream beds. It was fun to sit on the front seat of the boat with a stiff cane pole and a short line and drop a bonnett worm between the lily pads in the direction we caught the scent of fish spawning. When a bed was found it was easy to lift the fish straight up through the bonnetts with the stiff pole and short line which kept the line from wrapping around stems of the bonnetts. Our forays were highly rewarding—when we were lucky.

A fisherman never talks about the days he makes a waterhaul and how cramped he became sitting in one position in a boat. On one such occasion Sam confided in me that he was whipped out. Then he called my attention to a bunch of white ibis picking at the cows grazing in the water. The cows seemed to like the birds' attention.

While we were looking at this strange sight one of the cows started jumping up, standing on her hind legs and falling over backwards bellowing loudly the while. We pushed over and saw a jack fish about eighteen inches long which had struck the cow's tongue as she poked it out to gather the grass. The jackfish finally fell off of the cow's tongue but it came near drowning the cow.

Sam said, "That cow beat us fishing, it did catch a jack fish."

A limited formal education seemed only to add to Sam Jones's attractive personality and everyone was acquainted with him in that "neck of the woods." He was original and humorous and often preached in the little frame church about man's frailties. His text was always simple, just two or three words. As the members listened to him they may have doubted if his text was in the Bible, but he got through to his congregation because he preached from his heart. He often said "the greatest thing one can do for God or man is to pray!"

The subject of one of his sermons was "One Step," just "One Step," only two words. He spoke of one step to the right, one step to the left, one step forward and finally one step backward, but the last step in a man's life is the one step into eternity. How could anyone ever forget a simple sermon like that?

Come what may, every Sabbath day Sam and his family dressed in their "Sunday go to meeting clothes," piled in his old car and went to the little church where Sam held forth. One winter day enroute to church after a torrential rain, Sam stopped short of the creek bridge and inquired of a man if it was safe to cross the bridge during the high water.

The man replied confidently, "Sho, it'll hold you up." Sam said when he reached the middle of the bridge, "You know what that

Tommy Porter and "Bo" Jones with a fine catch of fish.

bridge went and done? It just 'squatted' and we all fell in the creek." Sam was the only casualty with a part of the bridge landing on his leg while the others scurried for safety.

After the accident the little country church was closed for a few weeks until a substitute preacher was secured at a much higher cost. That irritated Sam before he ever heard him preach.

The Sunday the new preacher arrived, Sam, with his family and his hound dog, "Blue," were in church to greet him. When the visiting parson started for the pulpit there was old Blue lying on the floor, stretched out full length, fast asleep, blocking the way. It was an embarrassing moment for the new minister as he tried to step over or around him but didn't succeed and finally hauled off and kicked old Blue. Old Blue, who had always been at home in the church, was so startled he yelped in alarm and sprang through an open window. Sam said, "That sho chawed me out and I couldn't listen to the sermon." The preacher apologized and Sam soon cooled off after he remarked that the only consolation he got out of the service was that old Blue was outside and didn't have to listen to the sermon.

No wonder the ushers at church gave this old dog a fond pat on the head when he appeared every Sunday. Two of the deacons borrowed old Blue one moonlight night and he treed a large 'possum which was no trouble to capture. However, they became tired of carrying the 'possum by the slick tail as was the custom and placed it in the little church until the next morning but completely forgot it. The 'possum in an effort to escape climbed up in the rafters directly over the spot where the preacher stood when he opened the service.

Sunday evening after the congregation sang the opening hymn, Sam, being the preacher, said, "Let us pray—Great God what a 'possum!" for as he glanced up he was startled by a frightened mammal a few feet over his head. Sam paused with the worship while the deacons removed the 'possum, then he apologized to the congregation.

After the sermon the deacons passed the four homemade wooden boxes through the congregation for the offertory, then marched down the aisle and presented the boxes to Sam for his blessing. After Sam looked at the nickels and pennies he was so disgusted he said, "Put the boxes to one side, that's not enough to bless." It was noticeable as the services continued the mannerisms of the preacher had changed because his accustomed glance upward to heaven had been replaced with a slight grin, but when the meeting was over all were forgiven and everyone seemed to be happy.

The officers of the little church were chiefly men who acted as caretakers of the hunting and fishing camps around Lake Iamonia and were expert hunters, fishermen and guides. Sam preached Sunday after Sunday on the Ten Commandments and the great joy of living with love in one's heart and hatred for no man. Sam never received any money for his efforts but the members brought him something of which they had— a bunch of turnip greens, a dressed chicken, the leg of a deer, a dozen eggs, pork chops, half dozen dressed squirrels, just anything they could spare and which Sam used to help feed his family.

During the spring of the year when the weather warmed up the boatmen around Lake Iamonia looked forward to "Preaching and dinner on the grounds." Each family brought a basket full of good food and spread it on a long, rough homemade table. There was always strong but friendly rivalry between the women as to who could bring the finest food.

When the "goodies" were piled on the table Sam rose to say a few spiritual words and pronounce the invocation. However, on one occasion he spoke impromptu and allowed his mind to wander. Sam was saying, "We must be thankful for God's bounties of love, just look at dat big dish of brown lake bream." One of the brothers said, "Amen."

Then Sam said, "Also, that heaping platter of fried spring chicken." Another brother cried out, "Amen and Amen."

"But that 'possum in the middle of the table stuffed with yellow yams, which the juice is oozing out of—." Sam didn't get any further because the crowd couldn't be held back and in the excitement one of the men threw a ripe tomato and hit a deacon in the face.

The deacon wiped the juice from his brow, jumped on a bench, held up his hands for silence and said, "Brothers and Sisters, go ahead and eat this fine lunch. After dinner I want Parson Sam to let us sing 'Nearer My God to Thee,' then pronounce the benediction. After which I invite you all to come down to the waterfront to see the damndest

Negro fight you ever heard of."

The guides around Lake Iamonia customarily gathered at the boat landings before day during the duck season and built a "fat wood" fire to keep warm while they talked. They discussed the arrival of the latest flight of Bullnecks which always preceded the freezing weather in the north and compared notes on the different locations where the ducks were feeding on the lake.

One of the boatmen said he had seen a drove of wild ducks after a long all night flight drop into the lake and immediately place their head underneath their wings and go to sleep, they were so fatigued.

All the men freely told of their experiences. Tat Brooks said the otters played around his blind acting like a passel of children playing hide and seek, and now and then swiping one of his ducks which had been shot down.

Before this group dispersed they usually mentioned some good deed of their preacher, whom they respected and followed because Sam Jones always got through to them and was their spiritual leader. Half of the guides were deacons in the church even though many of them could not read or write. Jimmy Fisher who stuttered asked if it was true that the church was buying a chandelier? He said, "If they do there is no one who can play it. What they needs is something which will give light." This kind of remark always kept the boatmen in a good humor.

Then Sam's latest sermon was mentioned, "Be ye wise as serpents and innocent as doves." One of the group said he never saw a wise rattlesnake, for if you step near one he may kill you. "I say beware of snakes they are dangerous as hell. Doves are nice birds."

This was a typical conversation heard by the boatmen around the early fire before day. All of which, sadly, is a thing of the past.

Sam Jones was a talented man who lived for others, he had God's blessing and he freely passed it on to everyone he contacted. Today a new church stands in the place of the former little frame sanctuary and is a monument which reminds everyone of the unselfish deeds of a strong Christian black man, my friend, Sam Jones.

Maron Gurley was a small wiry man whose long experience as a guide on Lake Iamonia caused him to be in demand by many hunters and fishermen seeking a talented boatman. He was in charge of Jack E. Ladson's camp and his services and allegiance was reserved for his boss, but he was at liberty to guide other hunters when unoccupied.

Maron, being treasurer of the little church, was kind and helpful to everyone, but he had a sporting streak in his make-up which caused him to live by a code of ethics all his own. To rig up a homemade still and run a little moonshine on a cold day was no sin to Maron as long as he did not sell it, so he often sat by a still hidden away in an isolated branch and when a cupful of hot "licker" slowly dropped out of the condenser, he drank it. He would select a day when the weather was not fit for man or beast, so he managed to hide his rascality.

The duck hunter fortunate enough to secure Maron as a guide was reasonably sure of getting the opportunity to bag the limit. Maron had the knack of locating the Ringnecks and quickly throwing up a temporary blind in their line of flight.

One cold morning Nat Williams had Maron for a boatman and the anticipation of an exciting hunt prompted him to challenge Maron to a proposition. Nat placed a bottle of bourbon whiskey between them and each had a pack of cigarettes. Every time a duck flew straight into Nat and he killed it he smoked a cigarette and took a swallow of bourbon, but every time he missed, Maron smoked a cigarette and took a swallow of whiskey. This seemed fair even though Maron knew Nat was a splendid duck shot, especially with them flying straight in, and he proved it by killing the first duck stone dead. Flipping out a cigarette, lighting it and taking a swallow of bourbon, Nat repeated this performance three straight times, but as he stood up and glanced down his gun barrel at the fourth duck Maron could not resist the temptation and rocked the boat with a motion of his body so well timed it was impossible to detect. Nat missed the next six shots while Maron passed out.

After Maron stretched out in the bottom of the boat, sound asleep, the boat became steady and Nat finished his duck limit, but he had a tough time pushing the boat to the landing.

Nat Williams was original, successful, and one of Thomasville's most unforgettable characters—a member of the Board of Education, City Council, Board of Trustees of Archbold Memorial Hospital and a great member of the Rotary Club. He was citizen of the year to many even though he lived long before this award was given.

One dark night when Nat and I were sitting in a little bateau at the mouth of East River, near the lighthouse at St. Marks waiting for the Ladd boat to pick us up, I said, "Nat, you are more interested in giving those in distress a hand than any friend I have."

"Well," he replied, "at sixteen I volunteered for World War I and during a battle I promised God if he would get me out alive I would kneel down every night of my life and say my prayers, and I would try to do something good for someone every day." This promise Nat kept the rest of his life.

The guides making a livelihood on the lakes between Thomasville and Tallahassee always displayed a personal interest in the hunters and fishermen they were accompanying.

How could one forget driving up to Jimmy Fisher's little cottage far back in the woods at 10 P. M. on a freezing damp night and asking him to hunt ducks at daylight? Eventually the wooden shutters of his cabin made a screeching noise and then came Jimmy's stuttering voice saying his jaw was swelled way up, but he would be ready come daylight to take my brother, Grover, on the lake.

Several generations have passed since a hunter sat quietly in a boat with a guide scanning the skies for ducks or seeking a place to fish. These "boatmen" were a group of individuals whose joy came from the satisfaction of having a good hunt or a successful catch of fish.

They had plenty to eat and did not worry about the things which drive people into a frenzy today. They always stood ready to help those in distress and possessed no hate. One could feel the sincere companionship which existed between a guide and a hunter even though few words were ever spoken.

Henry Vickers, one of the few surviving boatmen from our big lakes. Henry was born, and still lives, on what is now Tall Timbers Research Station.

This picture was made in memory of Majo and the other boatment of his era. They were a distinct breed—hardy, proud, generous, dependable and honest. They seemed to know instinctively the best locations for decoying in a duck or hooking a fish, and no effort was too much for them to get there. The contributions they made to the enjoyment of hunting and fishing on the big lakes was as priceless as it is irreplaceable.

Lake Iamonia provides recreation for many outdoor enthusiasts who live within motoring distance, and the array of camps on the north shore is evidence of the number of them who spend the night in order to be on the water

This picture was taken from the dam by
Tidwell's Studio and shows the lilies in the
spring and the shore line near the basin end
of Lake Iamonia. This view will probably
last for mankind until the end of time.

at daybreak. No such transient, though was
Scotie Beverley, who inherited Judge Luke's
camp at the west end of the lake and made
it his permanent home. He married and raised
his family on the banks of the lake he loved
so dearly.

Scotie was a living legend, known far and
wide for his exploits. About six feet tall, well
built but on the slender side, Scotie had the
exceptional coordination that all really great
natural athletes have. He was a phenomenal
wing shot, fine fisherman, champion golfer—
in fact, with seeming ease he excelled at any

sport he put his hand to. On top of that, he
had a keen, quick mind.

During the Second World War Scotie was
drafted by the Air Force to teach wing shooting, mainly on the skeet range, to turret
gunner trainees. Aside from that absence and
occasional brief periods when he had to work
to raise needed money, usually by making a
commission for selling a tract of land, he
lived on Lake Iamonia from 1927 to 1965,
hunting, fishing and studying the wildlife.

He was kind and helpful to man or beast.
I remember him splinting the broken leg of

a fox, nursing the animal back to health and then releasing it. He often entertained famous athletes such as Babe Ruth and Spurgeon Chandler, and in fact when Scotie's local friends had important visitors or guests they wanted to have the very best hunting, they usually asked Scotie to take them out. Some showed appreciation by paying a fee while others carried back with them all the game available, dressed and neatly packed, leaving only a handshake and a few kind words. However, Scotie was more interested in giving them a fine time than in getting money.

More than one person has told of sitting in a boat with Scotie Beverley and seeing him knock down five ducks from the single pass of a flight. An ever-ready bettor, his favorite wager back in the days before small bag limits was that he could bag twenty ducks out of a box of twenty-five shells. No one has ever claimed to have collected from him on that bet. On the lighter side, he would wager he could fire a shotgun into the air and catch the shot in his hunting cap. He used a twelve guage pump-gun, worked a shell into the barrel, removed it leaving the shell exposed, pulled the trigger igniting the powder with barely enough force to roll the shot into his hat.

One of Scotie's truest friends was W. C. (Bud) Vereen, a prominent south Georgia business man and avid outdoorsman, who often accompanied him on hunting and fishing trips. Mr. Vereen's quiet, unselfish disposition and Scotie's great skill with a gun and a flyrod sealed a lasting friendship.

On one occasion Scotie placed Bud on the front seat of a boat and pushed out to a duck blind where he arranged the decoys in a position which caused the ducks to fly in from right to left, thus giving them more freedom to follow through with their guns. The idea worked fine, but eventually two ducks sailed in from the opposite direction and Bud, from his cramped position, missed with both barrels. However, he glanced back in time to see both ducks fall at the sound of two shots and saw that Scotie had fired from his left shoulder even though he was right-handed.

A famous big game hunter, whose nationally exhibited movies showed his close encounters with ferocious wild animals, visited a Thomasville friend and was taken duck hunting on Lake Iamonia. It was one of those occasions when a Bullneck "knows where it is going," closes its wings and dives on the decoys, going like a flash and sounding like an approaching tornado. The noted hunter soon shot out of shells but bagged only two Bullnecks. Even so, he declared he enjoyed trying to hit them.

After the hunt the local sportsman drove by Scotie Beverley's house and introduced the celebrated hunter. Sizing up the situation without being told, Scotie promptly broke out a bottle of bourbon, and waited. Sure enough, when the celebrity's spirits revived he began to recite one after another of his harrowing jungle experiences, all to the great delight and fascination of Scotie's children. His prowess grew with each encounter, and when he described a barehanded escape from two man-eating tigers after his gun bearer had fled with his rifle, it was too much for Scotie, himself no slouch of a story teller.

Finally the mighty hunter ran out of breath and bourbon, and when he paused to replenish both, Scotie figured it was his turn. He said, "Last summer somebody stole my rifle, took it from the front porch. The next Saturday night about dark I went to the country store where all the boatmen trade, got down on my hands and knees where everybody could see me and made a lot of low, groany noises. 'Mr. Beverley, what are you doing?' one of the men asked but I said nothing. I set up a skull and crossbones, spilled gun powder all the way around it and waved my hands while I let the fire from my cigarette ignite the powder. Then I said, 'I am conjuring the man who stole my rifle.'

"That night about two o'clock a knock woke me up and a woman's voice said, 'Mr. Beverley, Jim sent your rifle back and asks you please goodness take the conjure off'n him.'

I asked if his hands were swelling. 'Yes sir.' Then I asked if his feet were swelling. 'Yes sir.' 'Does his head ache?' 'Yes sir.' 'Does his heart ache?' 'Yes sir.'

" 'Well, it's too late now, he will be dead in the morning. Always remember when Beverley makes a conjure there is no cure." Jim died that night and I haven't missed a thing since or locked the doors once."

As Scotie wound up his tale he noted that the celebrity was eyeing him narrowly and with a puzzled frown, but Scotie only blandly returned the gaze. Abruptly and with some haste the visitor rose, leaving his half-emptied drink, and suggested to the mutual friend that they leave.

Scotie Beverley lived as free as the air he breathed and was beholden to no man, always believing that God placed him on earth to enjoy every moment and to be of use to others. He may well have been this area's keenest observer of wildlife in modern times. Literally hundreds of local outdoorsmen—Vereen Bell, Bud Vereen, Bill Flowers, Babe White, Tom Mardre, Jim Campbell, Chris CoCroft, Tom Hawkins, Julien (Bull) Headley, just to mention a very few—prized his companionship and valued his advice. He

was easily one of the most unforgettable characters who lived in our midst.

Although in a "normal duck winter" tens upon tens of thousands of the fast flying, good eating wildfowl—enough to blacken the sky when they take wing—congregate on our big lakes, the local duck hunters are well aware of the dependence of this happy circumstance upon the conditions of the nesting grounds in the distant Canadian prairie marshes. Consequently, almost to the man they contribute to Ducks Unlimited.

As is well known, this worthy organization, working with the Canadian Government, has provided vast areas of wet lands and lakes for wild ducks to nest and to raise their broods. Innumerable dams have been built to hold back and store rainwater that would otherwise run off and permit dry, parched ground during spring and summer droughts. This may be the outstanding conservation undertaking of modern times, as it has created an ideal environment not only for ducks but for all the wildlife of the marshes.

Ducks Unlimited has erected several dams with local donations and made "Lake Thomasville," shown on the map below.

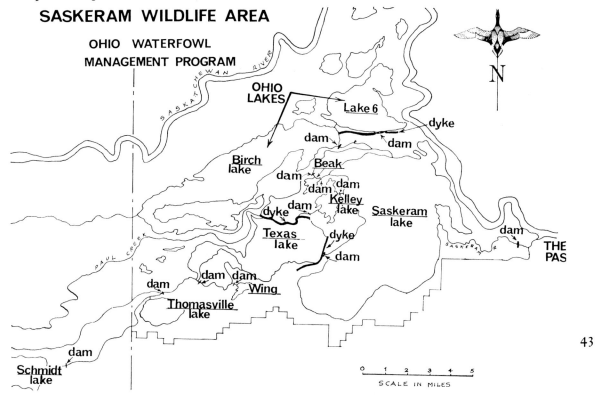

43

CHAPTER FIVE

Of the many kinds of game that abound in our area, deer and turkey are the largest and are probably the most difficult for the hunter to bag. No hunter slips up on either one—he must wait for them to come to him.

In the case of deer, two factors besides the animal's wariness contribute to the difficulty. The whitetail deer is found over practically all the eastern half of the United States, but in our section, unlike in other areas and even a hundred or so miles north of here, it generally feeds and ranges about only at night and stays bedded down through the day. Then, there are plenty of swamps, some impenetrable, sloughs and thickets for the deer to bed down in.

Nighthunting, or jack-lighting deer, is strictly forbidden by law and full effort is made to enforce that restriction. But the law hands out as well as withholds, and the handout in this instance is permitting the hunting of deer with dogs. There's reason for that, as otherwise just about no deer would be killed and it is our only game animal with no natural predator to hold down its population growth. Then the law tacks on a further restriction: no high-powered rifles, only shotguns and buckshot.

Thus, a deer hunt becomes a special event —it hardly can be a casual or a singlehanded undertaking. Depending upon the size of the area to be hunted out, or driven, a dozen to a hundred or so men are needed to stand at stations preferably on the perimeter of the area. One or more packs of hounds, each numbering from a half dozen to thirty or more dogs, accompanied by their owners and a helper or two, afoot or horseback, search out, beat and comb the area.

As might be expected, more often than not a good deal of commotion ensues—frenzied hounds barking, yelping, howling, and yowling, the drivers whooping and spurring them on to still greater effort, guns booming in many directions. A stranger might readily wager that a hunter's risk of getting shot is alarmingly high, but the exact opposite is the case. In fact, such casualties are totally unheard of locally, while if news reports are to be believed about as many hunters and domestic livestock as deer are killed each season in the dogless deer-hunting sections.

It should be added that surprisingly few deer are killed on our deer drives. Even with periodic open seasons on does, deer get more plentiful each year and they can be unbelievably destructive to farm crops.

Good hounds—hard hunting, keen nosed, fleet footed—being essential for a successful drive, the outstanding packs become known far and wide, and are much in demand. One of the best, all well-trained Walker hounds, was owned by J. E. Ladson, an ardent deer hunter who was invited to drives all over North Florida and South Georgia. It was a treat to accompany him on a deer drive even though I wasn't interested in the shooting. Jack had the ability to stay up with the dogs on foot while it took my best to keep up on horseback.

Just to sit in the saddle and watch the strike dog work a trail, carefully sniffing the ground as he trotted along, searching in one direction and another, then finally catch a faint scent and make an indifferent, cold-trail yelp, was interesting. Eventually the scent would become stronger and stronger and all the dogs join in with furious barking, until the entire pack sounded like one great chorus. Soon the hounds would begin jumping up in the air, bouncing like rubber balls, turning their heads from side to side trying to get a glimpse of the deer they expected to spring from the ground. Jack was usually with the dogs and at times had a shot when the deer jumped.

If the deer evaded Jack the dogs were smart enough to see it and make a frantic sight race until they were outdistanced. Even though the dogs would lose sight of the deer the trail was so hot they packed in the chase, barking loud and clear as they drove the deer toward the standers. This was an exciting moment for the hunters who expected momentarily to see the deer flash into sight and afford a shot. Often the deer would get through the ring of standers, who then stood listening to the voices of their favorite hounds.

If the deer was killed the dogs stopped, but if it evaded the standers the hounds continued to run until Jack Ladson blew them in with his cowhorn which they could hear for miles. Many times the pack of Walker hounds would jump a deer in the morning and continue to run until midnight.

I remember sitting on a pony overlooking a branch head and seeing a large doe lope out of the brush in plain view of a pack of trained hounds and lead them away, far beyond the sound of their voices. Eventually the same doe doubled back and got her fawn, evading the entire group of dogs, which showed the protective instinct and cunning bravery this mother deer had for its young.

An occasion like this would make any sportsman glad that deer have some tricks that enable them to survive.

Harry Wyche, a grandson of one of the early settlers of Thomas County, was a great sportsman who gave an annual deer drive for his friends on the Blackshear Plantation which belonged to his wife's family. The Blackshear property comprised several thousand acres of farm land which had been idle since the Civil War and had grown into a vast forest.

This property was bordered on the south by "Susina," a "forest plantation" of ten thousand acres owned by James S. Mason. Several generations of Masons were born and raised at Susina and they used their influence, talent and money to make our section a better place to live in. The people of Thomasville loved and esteemed the Masons because they were so unselfish, always working in the hospital, church, and with those in need.

The first wild turkeys seen near Thomasville in modern times was a small drove on Susina which Jim Mason thought so much of he hired a special man to guard it. From this small start and careful protection wild turkeys spread over just about the whole area between Thomasville and Tallahassee, Florida.

Deer were very numerous on Susina and the Blackshear place back in the '30s, and when Harry Wyche scheduled a deer drive, Jim Mason always cooperated by assisting in any way a good neighbor could.

Mac Morrow, who lived near Auburndale, Florida, had another outstanding pack—perhaps the fastest hounds I have ever seen. When Mac opened the dog-box door they hit the ground running and ran wide open whether hunting, trailing or chasing. Sometimes Mac came up for the drives, but Jack Ladson, living much nearer, was there more often. With either one, an exciting drive was assured.

Harry Wyche invited all his friends so a huge crowd was always on hand. Perhaps the two most noteworthy characters were Tom Mardre and Bud Blackshear.

Tom Mardre was an athletically built, quick moving man with a lot of dash and style of his own who never played second fiddle and "took no slack talk from any man living." He was fiercely independent, born and raised in the saddle and he knew his way around in the woods. Harry let Tom Mardre ramrod the hunts and he always brought chitterlings and had his helper, Adam, cook them for lunch. All real deer hunters supposedly longed for a mess of hot hog chitterlings for lunch and when there were more hunters than chitterlings Tom Mardre sprinkled a few grains of corn in the frying pan to slow down the appetite of the hunter to make them go around. I can't stand the thought or taste of chitterlings, but when you are with a group of outdoorsmen you don't complain and eat whatever is offered with a show of relish.

Bud Blackshear, who was reared on the Blackshear Plantation, had a native dry wit and without trying was highly amusing. He was a naturalist at heart and spent long hours studying the birds and wild animals of the woods.

Bud claimed that all the creatures of the woods were frightened by sudden motion but they were not scared of a man and he proved it by sitting still in the open while wild turkey, deer, quail, 'coons, etc. fed within a few feet of him.

Many times Bud sat around at lunch and entertained the hunters with his stories and quaint expressions. He said he got out of bed every morning when the cook hit the grits spoon three times as it was a sure signal breakfast was ready to serve.

Bud wasn't all talk. On one occasion I saw him catch a blacksnake with his bare hands, whirl it around like a whip and pop his head off, the same as if a sharp knife had severed it from its body. He described watching a king snake hunt down a rattlesnake and then slowly squeeze it to death. He is one of the few men I have ever known who witnessed such a contest.

He also told of watching a male and female rattlesnake mate as he sat in a turkey blind made of myrtle bush branches. The snakes made love by raising their bodies two feet

"Bo" Jones shows off the handsome rack of an old buck.

or more straight up in the air and scraping and rubbing against each other.

The lunch period when everyone gathered and talked was the highlight of the organized deer hunt during the period of 1925 to 1950. The rules which have been handed down from one generation to the other continue to govern a deer hunt and are simple but strictly observed.

Deer have increased greatly in the Albany, Thomasville and Tallahassee area. The large estates protect the game and the vast number of acres planted in young pine trees furnish good refuge the year around.

Many of the land owners give their neighbors and friends a well organized deer drive once or twice a year. The deer meat is divided among all the hunters participating, so everyone is rewarded. Each man has his own recipe for preparing venison which he thinks is the best—certainly no two of them are exactly alike. However, there is one idea they all agree on. When a deer is killed after a very long chase the meat is really tough unless it is skinned in the woods and hung in a refrigerated room to age.

A deer is the most graceful wild animal in our forest. If one could only see in slow motion the ease with which a big buck throws his head back while carrying his antlers through the thick brush as he glides effortless along, they would never forget.

Most woodsmen claim a deer has the keenest eyes of any game in the woods, yet they never look upward and a stand built twenty-five feet high in a tree gives one a chance to get a perfect picture or study their habits. Their instinct is unbelievable as they watch the small birds playing around and have no fear of advancing without caution. However, if there is no sign of life around they stand still until they are convinced there is nothing to harm them.

Many times when a hunter kills a buck in the presence of a doe, the doe will run off fifty or one hundred yards and stamp her feet hoping to attract the buck, "the same as calling, come on." A game warden said he sat in his jeep and saw a doe put her fawn over a wire fence. Certainly the mother risks her life without thinking day after day. Just about all hunters draw the line when it comes to shooting a doe with a fawn.

My last deer hunt occurred at Walterboro, South Carolina, on the large Bradley Estate, as a guest of Mac Morrow. I had looked forward to participating in the drive in this vast forest where the game was protected and plentiful. We were taken in jeeps to the deer stands which were spaced about a quarter of a mile apart, assuring every one there was no danger from a stray shot. When the guide stopped the jeep and looked at me he said, "This is a good deer crossing." And I was left standing with my gun.

I saw I was in a deep hammock containing many varieties of large hardwood trees which had shaded out the brush permitting vision for a long distance. I felt at home among the beautiful giant trees and soon became relaxed as I sat down by an old beech whose trunk was half hollowed out from age. Leaning back in the cavity of this tree with my legs stretched out on the ground brought me the comfort required to remain motionless for a long period of time and gave me a view of any approaching game. It was early in the fall of the year and the leaves had turned every color in the rainbow after losing their chlorophyll. Just waiting and resting in this quiet surrounding seemed to bring me peace, hard to describe.

A quotation kept returning to me: "Be still and know that I am God." I wondered if I understood this meaning, when a motion attracted my attention and there stood a four point buck. I instinctively reached for my gun and the deer jumped five feet high as I fired. Only one buckshot hit him, breaking his vertebra and paralyzing his body. As I approached he threw back his handsome head, focused his beautiful, frightened eyes on me and died. I have never shot another deer.

CHAPTER SIX

The beautiful rivers in south Georgia and northwest Florida meander one way, then another, sometimes making a course like the letter "S," but eventually flow into the Gulf of Mexico. During flood stages, water covers the low adjoining areas but soon recedes causing ideal conditions for hardwood to thrive, forming open hammocks abounding in large game such as deer, wild turkeys, 'coons, opposum, squirrels, wildcat, bear and panthers. The rivers usually have a high bluff where pine trees grow opposite the low hammocks. All of these streams follow the contour of the land, changing directions at every bend. It is easy to imagine how these natural habitats furnished plenty of game and fish for the Indians and early settlers.

After the Indians were removed many men seeking food and recreation have enjoyed these fresh water streams. It cost very little to cut a reed pole with a pocket knife and attach a homemade line or to punch a few air holes in a dried gourd and fill it with grasshoppers which had gone to roost in tall dogfennels at sunset. All of these simple preparations were exciting to a local fisherman planning to be at the river come daybreak. No sport is any more exciting to us Crackers than waiting at the river bank to hear the first chirp of a swamp bird, then noticing a flight of wood ducks passing over-

head and, one by one, hearing all the sounds of wildlife entering into a big crescendo. Now is the moment to bait your hook with a kicking grasshopper and lower it in the water without a sinker and witness a big red-belly strike. Only those who have had this kind of experience appreciate the fun and recreation of catching a string of red-bellies and cooking them on the river banks.

Allie Robinson, Lewis Wilson and I were among the first men in our area to successfully use a fly rod and we spent many hours casting in the rivers south of Thomasville and Tallahassee. The fish had never seen an artificial fly and were easy to catch on a Royal Coachman or Black Gnat retrieved behind a small spinner.

The only accident I recall was catching Lewis Wilson in the ear lobe on a long backcast as he was quietly drifting by without my noticing him. My pliers and iodine fixed this.

The three of us secured guides on the Ochlocknee River near Sopchoppy, Florida. My boatman, Ben Isler, had his boat full of fishing poles and a gallon can of earthworms. I said, "Ben, I use a flyrod and won't have any use for these poles, bait, etc." He replied, "These fish won't strike a fly." But he finally cleared the boat and we motored three miles up the river and started drifting back on the shaded side of the stream. It was early in the morning and I greased my line, causing it to float, and attached a top fly to the leader. I could see that Ben was in a sullen mood—he did not say a word when I asked him to keep the boat a good distance from the banks. However, he watched me play the line out into the air and gently drop the fly in the dark water, a foot from the bank, and a big red-belly struck before the line splashed into the water. This was too much and Ben shouted, "Damn, look at that fish fight."

I was landing a fish on almost every cast and suddenly realized Ben was in a happy frame of mind, enjoying the fun as much as I was.

When we pulled up to a landing at noon to cook our dinner, Allie and Lewis reported good luck. While we were all seated watching the bream fry in deep oil, Ben stood up and faced us with these words: "This morning taught me never to drown another worm!"

Fish seem to have a way of keeping all men modest. Well do I remember inviting the Thomasville Fire Department to a fish fry on the Ochlocknee River to thank them for their outstanding work.

Five expert fly rod fishermen guaranteed to catch the fish for the occasion and met at the "Ten Acre Hole" six miles south of Thomasville on the Ochlocknee River near daybreak. Three of us went down the stream and two in the opposite direction, leaving a space of several bends between the eager nimrods. After four hours of constant fishing I had three small stump knockers and this discouraging result caused me to become impatient, almost panicky, at the thought of making a "water haul." I was sure my buddies were having the same hard luck and time was running out. How could our few fish feed the multitude? Only a miracle could happen to produce the fish.

Glancing down the river I saw a tall local character as "barefooted as a yarddog" wading toward me, casting with a long reed pole sufficient to reach the dark, deep holes on the opposite side of the stream. He had a string of bream as long as his leg tied to his belt and dangling in the running water to keep them fresh. I could hardly believe my eyes and was careful to approach him with modesty.

"What are you fishing with?" I asked. "Gator fleas," he replied. When I said, "Gosh, I never saw one," he put down his pole and showed me a hellgrammite taken from the decayed trees in the river and explained that fish would strike them in preference to any other bait. Eventually I told him of our poor luck and he untied his long string of fish and gave them to me for the Firemen's fish fry, without compensation. I was overcome by his kindness and generosity, but I had learned that folks in the woods seldom sold game or fish because these were God's gifts to mankind and should be shared with others. The act of the river fisherman was typical and my act of tying the string of fish to my belt, giving my buddies the impression I had caught them, was the typical deception of a town fisherman.

It was such a relief to have the fish I failed to ask the name of the river fisherman, but upon my next visit to this spot there he was with the same equipment, long pole, gator fleas, and fish dangling from his belt, wading the river. "Hey!" I cried. He paused and answered, "Hey, yourself."

Then I commented, "The river is real low."

He replied, "Why it's so low you could bite it in two and drink up the upper half." He continued, "I was out here fishing the other day, just dropping here, there, and the other, hoping to catch a perch, but couldn't get a nibble so I cut through the woods looking for a likely spot. I had no socks on to speak of and felt something tugging at my heelstrings and thought it was a bamboo brier. I glanced over my shoulder and bless God it had ten rattles and a button."

"What did you do?"

"Why I pulled my jacknife out of my jeans, cut him loose and sliced off a piece the size of your hand, slapped it over the bite and haven't told Papa or Mammy about it yit."

While he was narrating his story it dawned on me that this had to be Tom Avery. After a good laugh I said, "I know who you are!" He replied, "You do? Well who are you?" This is the way we became friends.

Tom made a living before automobiles by hauling salt mullet in a covered wagon from the Gulf of Mexico during the fall of the year when these fish were running and full of roe. On Saturdays he would back his rig up against the sidewalk curb on Jackson Street in Thomasville and retail the fish.

A customer once inquired if he prepared the salt mullet and he replied, "Yes, I am not so good at gutting 'em, but when it comes to heading 'em I take it from no man."

Tom carried a string of catfish, which he caught mudding in a slough, into Thomas Drug Store where the town big-wigs and the plantation owners gathered to swap stories. Dr. Thomas said, "Tom, that is a mighty fine string of cats, what will you take for them?" "I dunno, what you give me?" replied Tom. When Dr. Thomas said fifteen cents and snickered, Tom realized he was making fun of his fish and said, "You must be crazy. My old lady hain't lost her taste for cats and I'll take 'em to her."

Tom possessed more than a Cracker accent and original humor. His reputation to do a simple kindness for those in need or distress (like giving me all his fish) was known to all. He was one in a generation.

The Ochlocknee River begins near Sylvester, Georgia, and flows in a southwesterly direction into the Gulf of Mexico at Panacea, Florida. On its way to the Gulf this beautiful clear stream with sand bars and high bluffs on every other side winds its course within a few miles of the towns of Moultrie, Ochlocknee, Cairo, Thomasville and other towns until it crosses the Florida boundary line west of Tallahassee. There a power dam has been erected to furnish electricity which is used by the city of Tallahassee. The backwater forms Lake Talquin, a noted fishing area.

Ochlocknee is an Indian word, meaning crooked waters, and how appropriate the definition is because the river makes untold bends in its winding route southward. Most of the land the river flows through from Thomasville to Lake Talquin is divided into large tracts owned by individuals who protect and encourage the propagation of game.

In the fall of the year when the first frost appears and the trees along the river banks begin to color, it is a great experience to pack the bare necessities required to camp and fish, along with a .22 rifle and a camera in a small boat, put into the river near Cairo and leisurely scull down the Ochlocknee with a companion who loves the outdoors. Many times you are surprised, as the boat quietly drifts around a bend in the river, to see a bunch of wild turkeys or a deer standing on a sand bar drinking from the clear stream. There is not a spare moment for either man in the boat as one is sculling from the back seat as the other casts a fly or spinning lure in a likely place to hook a red-belly bream or large-mouth bass. Both men must stay on the lookout for hidden snags or portions of fallen trees in the stream. After a few days experience in the river they become accustomed to sounds which at first startle them, such as a raft of wood ducks making a quick-get-away as they jump straight up off the water squalling like a boy getting a licking.

There are periods in the day when the birds, game and fish seem to be resting or taking a nap. Not a sound can be heard or the movement of a single creature seen, and the stillness closes in as the boat drifts downstream. The rest periods are eventually broken by the sound of a woodpecker or the barking of a squirrel. Soon the big owls hoot a few times and that is the same as if a dinner bell had sounded—everything in the woods begins to move. Such experiences teach one to move quietly and listen to the sounds of the forest. Most of the revelations in life come when we are alone and quiet.

Trips down the Ochlocknee River are not always easy, pleasant outings. Well do I remember one time, about when my voice was changing, Vallie Hawthorne and I packed our fishing tackle, frying pan, sleeping bags and small rifle in the middle of a light boat and put into the river at Waldens Bridge. For two days the weather was beautiful and we enjoyed every moment. On the second night after a dinner of red-bellies and corn bread "all hell broke aloose" as the river men say.

Our tent blew down and we were scared to death and soaking wet, but our first thought was one of the quickest and soundest decisions of our lives for we pulled our boat out of the water to keep the flash flood from carrying it away. Then we turned it upside down and crawled under it with our sleeping bags and became completely quiet. The lightning was fierce and we were praying to God to defend us from all the dangers and perils of that scary night. This was the first moment in my life that I realized I was entirely on my own, no mortal could help us and how natural it was for us to turn to God in help.

It was quiet in the darkness under that boat but each had an idea what the other was doing.

This wasn't, of course, as impressive a conversion as St. Paul's but the experience strengthened our faith in God which has been a continuing comfort. The rain and lightning cleared the atmosphere, the morning brought forth a beautiful day and we happily packed our boat and pushed off down stream. The fish refused to strike in the muddy water and for three days we ate squirrels shot with the little .22 rifle. Looking back, I am reminded of the old saying, "there is a time when the men are separated from the boys."

Today a few brave ones continue to take boat trips down the Ochlocknee but upon arriving in Lake Talquin they haul the boat by truck to a landing in the river below the dam. From the dam to Sopchoppy there are thousands of acres of land which belongs to the U.S. Government and large paper companies. Although, there are small plots along the river owned for generations by families who make a living renting boats, acting as guides, operating beehives which produce excellent tupelo honey, raising hogs that survive on acorns, beech nuts and the wild food of the river swamp. Some of the men who were born and raised on the Ochlocknee and own their landings are Mr. Cox, Meady Chasen, Alton Langston, Revels, Ted Roberts, Jack Langston, Hamp Langston and his brother, John Langston. All are highly responsible and fine persons.

It is a great treat to have dinner at one of these homes and I have seen venison, bear meat, wild turkey and fish served at one meal. Most of those who want a days outing on the Ochlocknee engage a boatman from one of the mentioned landings. Many times I have had the pleasure of fishing at these places with Tom Harlow, Jim and Corlene Campbell, Nat Williams, Bill Flowers, Jack Turner, Lewis Wilson, Allie Robinson, Dr. Bill Thomas, Forrest Knapp and many other Thomasville fishermen. They are among the finest fly fishermen and most interesting sportsmen who ever visited the Ochlocknee River.

Nat Williams may not have been the best fisherman, but he was great company and perhaps the best outdoor cook who ever made "muldouglass" in an iron pot. Nat often went to New York for his picture show business and while there shopped at the delicatessen stores for new ingredients to add to his muldouglass. Nothing in this world is as tasty to a fisherman as red belly bream taken from a live-box, dressed and fried in deep oil on the river bank. When Nat shouted "come and get it" he waited for only one thing, the blessing. He never forgot that he had promised God if his life was spared while fighting a battle in France he would always remember to give thanks for all the blessings that came his way.

Then there was Jim and Corlene Campbell. Jim was manager of Foshalee Plantation, owned by R. L. Ireland and Dave S. Ingalls, and was as knowledgeable of the ways of wildlife as anyone going. Once in a while, though not often, he was accompanied on our fishing trips by his wife Corlene whom Jim had taught to handle a gun and flyrod very skillfully. She was always most agreeable and added to our outing when present.

On one of our regular trips the men fished hard and made only a water haul. We drove back tired, hungry and worn out. When we arrived at Jim's home it was midnight but he made us come in, then awakened Corlene and she cooked scrambled eggs, bacon and toast. Corlene was a little disgruntled—not because she was disturbed from her slumber but because we had not taken her with us. No one could forget her many kindnesses.

After the fishing group had been organized for a while W. H. (Bill) Flowers was invited to join and he made a great addition. Flyrod fishing was a new sport to Bill while the other men were experienced, acquainted with all the tricks. The handicap did not dampen his enthusiasm, for Bill has the innate ability to accomplish anything he tries. He is a close observer who asks many questions.

On one occasion Bill was drifting down the river with his guide, carefully keeping his boat the proper distance from the bank to cast a fly. My guide was handling my boat in the same manner on the opposite side. The harder Bill and I tried to get a strike the more discouraged we became so finally I rigged up my secret weapon. Business immediately picked up. As I fed my line out downstream a grown red-belly would latch on and give me a great play in the swift water.

Bill and his boatman were watching—understandably because I was shouting, "Look, Bill, at that red-belly trying to pull this rod out of my hand!" Finally Bill said, "Crankup the motor, Hamp, let's get away from here.

You're watching Mr. Balfour and pushing me up in the limbs of these willow trees."

Just as far as I could hear Hamp's motor sputter it was carrying Bill away from me and after everything quieted down I grinned at the thought of chasing one of my fishing buddies out of the river.

But Bill had made a study of my technique with a flyrod. He acquired the same equipment—even our tackle boxes were alike, and he learned to wait on his line in making a long cast. Nevertheless I continued to out-fish him on almost every trip.

All fishermen are alike—when they reach the river there is a wild scramble to get in a boat and wet a line. In this moment of haste Bill accidentally placed my tackle box in his boat, cranked-up the motor and kicked down the river. When he opened what he thought was his tackle box for a fly there appeared equipment he had never seen. In one corner was a small paste board container with air holes punched in it, full of wild black crickets.

Then it dawned on him that he had my tackle box and by accident had discovered my "secret weapon." Bill had learned to fish with crickets long before he ever saw a flyrod and he landed a string of bream that put my day's work to shame.

While we were enjoying dinner Bill explained in detail how I had smuggled crickets in my tackle box and failed to share them with my good friends. On the next trip, we were eating when Nat Williams rose and, to get out attention, announced that Uncle John Langston, who was throwing his fish bones on the ground under his feet, had just reached down grabbed a little wild boar and castrated him all with one motion and we'd better watch and stay out of his reach.

Then Nat presented me with a clear plastic fishing box which could be examined without removing the top, and declared if any more "secret weapons" were found I had to share them. Nat finished his speech with these

52

The scenic Ochlocknee River. Fishermen willingly contend with the overhanging trees to catch the river's special red-breast bream.

words, "Bob, we trust you, we consider you one of the finest Christian gentlemen in all of Thomasville. But when you get in a fishing boat you are a grand scoundrel."

Bill Flowers seconded the motion and he was given a certificate assuring him he was a full-fledged member of our group.

Our outings on the Ochlocknee River furnished priceless moments of relaxation. Jim Campbell, a witty, razor-sharp "country boy" was at his best when telling political stories of his native state of Alabama. One of these dealt with two men who were running a hot, neck-and-neck race for office. One of the candidates hired a group of hecklers to sit in the city auditorium and everytime his opponent made a point the hecklers would interrupt with loud cries, "Yes, but tell us about your illegitimate children."

Finally the speaker was so harassed he stopped. When the audience became quiet he turned to the hecklers and pointed his finger and said, "You want to know about my illegitimate children so I will tell you. I loved that little girl and she bore me four children. I married her and gave those children my good name. I educated each one of them, sending them to college and they are going to be fine citizens. Now, you little hickory-headed s.o.b.s, you tell me what you have done for your children?" This open honest statement elected the candidate by a large majority.

On special occasions Major Louis Beard and Capt. "Babe" White motored down and joined our fishing group in time to partake of one of Nat Williams' famous meals served on the banks of the Ochlocknee River. Only those with a knowledge and love of the outdoors could appreciate an occasion the like of this. There was Babe White, who had traveled, hunted and fished all over the world, entering into the fun by telling of some hair-raising encounter he'd had with a fierce wild animal while hunting big game.

Major Beard noticed the native boatmen stretched out on the ground, their shoulders propped up against a swamp pine or oak tree, relaxing after a hard morning's work skulling a boat for us on the river. Each boatman had a paper plate full of red-bellies and hushpuppies. However, when Major Beard told of the most honest poacher he had ever encountered all the men stopped eating, straightened up and listened intently.

Major's story was true and told like this: "You fellows who live on the river and own your own property know how difficult it is to protect the wild game. One night a man phoned me and said, 'I'm putting you on notice. Tomorrow in the morning I am coming into your place and I'll kill one of your wild turkeys.' It was an open challenge and I gathered as many men as possible to prevent the poaching. Shortly after daylight a shot was heard and the search started, but eventually given up without any results. As the men were leaving they saw a hunter with a gun under his arm and a wild turkey slung over his shoulder sauntering down the middle of the public road. That was their man."

Someone in our party said, "Major, what did you do?"

"Well," he replied with a shrug, "it's not against the law to walk down the public road."

Major Beard wisely became a friend of this remarkable woodsman, retaining him as game warden and bird dog handler and he worked under Gordon Simmons for thirty years. His name was Clifton Felix Floyd, but all the local people knew him as "Spot" Floyd, one of the greatest shots and dog handlers in our quail country.

Spot was an asset to Greenwood. How well do I remember Spot calling me one night about eleven o'clock and saying, "Mr. Bob, I am going to handle the dogs in the morning. You, Price Headley and Major Beard will be shooting. I have told them you are the greatest quail shot living. So please don't you let me down!" He was keenly concerned for the dogs, the hunters and everyone involved. There was never but one "Spot."

Major Beard loved south Georgia and endeared himself to everyone he came in contact with, readily giving assistance and showing a spirit of kindness and cooperation. His love for this section was demonstrated when he remarked to me at his stag dinner party a few nights before he died, "This is a happy day for me because I have secured permission to be buried in the old cemetery at Greenwood."

In the stillness of the moment when his body was being lowered into the grave everyone stood with hat in hand, head lowered, while a big cock quail some few yards away on a dark weather stained stump whistled "Bob White" as if its heart would break, commemorating the passing of a friend to all Georgia Crackers.

Two of undoubtedly the most interesting men in America made their homes in Thomasville during the 1930s—Capt. H. A. White and Major Louis A. Beard.

Babe White was a grand looking man, standing six feet, seven inches tall and weighing over three hundred well proportioned pounds. He had been All American tackle at Syracuse University, gold medal winner on the Olympic team, guide and organizer of big game hunting in Africa. He had traveled all over the world and should have lectured on the stage.

Major Louis A. Beard, a West Pointer with great army experience, a polo player and a man of wide acquaintance, came to Thomasville to manage Greenwood Plantation, being connected with Payne Whitney and later with J. H. Whitney.

CHAPTER SEVEN

Stephen Foster's song, "The Old Folks at Home," made the Suwannee River known to everyone in America—even though few were aware of its location or know that the Suwannee was the boundary between the Timucua and Apalachee Indian tribes when north Florida was first explored. At that early time it was called Guasaca Equi, meaning "River of Reeds." The present name is thought to be a Negro corruption of San Juanee, meaning "little St. John."

The truly beautiful Suwanee River rises in the Okefenokee Swamp in south Georgia and empties in the Gulf of Mexico twenty-two miles south of Cross City, Florida. Only thirty-five miles of the river's course is in Georgia and as it flows southward through Florida it receives the water of the Withlacoochee, Alapaha and Santa Fe Rivers. The Suwanee Sound has many inlets and bays, and it is recorded that the pirates used these places as rendezvous points about 1780 to bury their treasure.

Those who have chartered Fred and Palmer Ladd's boat at St. Marks and cruised down the coastline to the mouth of the Suwannee have without fail appreciated the beauty of the river and the Gulf of Mexico. The Ladd Brothers were among the first who catered to fishing parties for overnight outings. Their boats would sleep eight or ten and everyone felt safe in their care, as they had navigated the Gulf for miles around.

Fred was the skipper of the boat which took Roscoe Fleetwood, W. W. Upchurch, Tom Mardre, Allie Robinson, Nat Williams and the writer to the Suwannee Sound. As we arrived at our destination, Fred Ladd pointed out the wreckage of a battered boat and explained that it was an old Confederate supply ship that the Union gun boats sank during the Civil War to block the channel.

We dropped anchor about four P. M. and everyone was restless to get in one of the bateaux, which was towed from St. Marks, and start fishing. Most of the men fished around the wreckage and caught a fine string of sea trout, but Tom Mardre and I kicked up one of the inlets to fish for fresh water bass.

The water up the river was noticeably dark which indicated it had originated in the Okefenokee Swamp. The trees grew close to the banks on both sides and caused deep shade on the water, a perfect place to play a "cripple minnow." After leaving the brackish water we fished for two hours thinking every cast would land a bass, but learned the hard way that the bass were not feeding. Completely exhausted and disgusted the motor was cut and the boat drifted with the stream. The sun had disappeared when we landed our first fish, but for the next thirty minutes a bass latched onto our lure on very near every cast until it became too dark to see.

Arriving at the Ladd boat with a fine catch and a full moon showing in the East we were in the humor to sing "way down upon the Suwannee River."

Tom Mardre was a fine companion who was at home in the woods and could handle a gun or fishing tackle with the most expert. He was resourceful, quick, experienced and had the knowledge it required to manage Greenwood Plantation.

Tom always went in great style and comfort and our cruise to the Suwannee was no exception, because he was accompanied by his efficient and faithful helper, Adam, who cooked a big black pot of mulligan stew which consisted of fish, onions, beans, pepper and more pepper. It required a man in perfect health to partake of this outdoor dish but I can vouch it was good. Every fisherman should make this trip to the Suwannee Sound.

The headwaters of the Suwannee, the Okefenokee Swamp, is forty miles long, twenty miles wide and the second largest swamp in the United States. It consists of approximately 400,000 acres and is more of a watershed than a swamp. The name Okefenokee is a Seminole Indian name meaning "Land of Trembling Earth." When the guides are conducting a group into the swamp they often jump on a floating island and show how the land shivers.

Vereen Bell, a Thomasville author, in his novel, "Swamp Water," gives an excellent description of this silent sanctuary where nature has not been disturbed.

Liston Elkins describes the Okefenokee in these words: "The pond cypresses are hung with streamers of gray moss that trail into the water or to the ground, tangling with vines and underbrush. Many of the boatruns cut into the thickness of the jungle growth at hidden entrances. Inside the cavernous swamp, the sun is often blotted out, giving an effect of twilight. Beautiful white blooms of red bay, loblolly bay and those of white bay and magnolia are silhouetted against the dark green foliage of the swampland. In the lower growth are honeysuckle, titi, hoorah bushes, red and black bamboo, bullace grapes, huckleberry, white alder, gallberry, haws and many other forms of trees and plant life."

It is a wonderful experience to quietly drift around in a small boat and see the wild birds, alligators, black bear, wildcats, snakes, lizards and other creatures of nature. Everyone returns from the Okefenokee with a different but profound impression of the encounter with nature. As a young man during 1920 I camped in the swamp one night and had to completely cover my body with wet moss to keep the mosquitoes from eating me up. However, these insects are not carriers of malaria.

The Suwannee River emerges from the Okefenokee on the southern extremity at Fargo.

We are not sufficiently appreciative of the beautiful rivers which furnish much recreational pleasure to the people of south Georgia and north Florida. We travel over the highways at such fast speed we hardly see them.

The Alapaha River is one of the favorite fishing streams. Recently canoeing has become popular on this interesting stream, which is lined with many varieties of hardwood trees. The Alapaha is 130 miles long, rising near Vienna, Georgia, and uniting with the Suwannee River in Hamilton County, Florida.

It has a comparatively small watershed because the Withlacoochee and Satilla Rivers crowd the Alapaha and drain waters that arise within a short distance of the latter stream. In rainy periods the Alapaha overflows and floods the low marginal swamps which border its course. In dry seasons it almost stops running except for a little trickle between the deep holes. With the white sand bars exposed it has been called a "bleached skeleton of a giant snake."

There are many explanations of the word

"Alapaha" but most people living near the river prefer to believe the word is derived from the Creek Indian word, "Helpata," meaning alligator.

Dr. John Archbold McCrea was one of the first doctors to practice medicine in Tifton, Georgia, and there he gave his long, useful life to caring for the people of that area. The doctors of that time drove a horse and buggy over a rough dirt road, often at night to deliver a baby or assist one in distress. There were no modern hospitals or government aid and the doctor's charges were small—many times they were paid only small gifts or "kind deeds." Yet, Dr. McCrea raised a family of five boys and two girls, giving each a college education and leaving them a heritage of eternal thankfulness from the community he served.

Dr. McCrea, like all doctors, was overworked at times to the breaking point, so he organized a hunting camp on the Alapaha River where he relaxed with his friends and family. Dr. McCrea's son, Henry, today a prominent citizen of Thomasville, recalls as a teenage boy he was fishing in a quiet lagoon connected with the Alapaha, when suddenly a great commotion began on the river bank. Only a few yards away an alligator, eight feet long, was slipping down the slick bank headed for him.

Henry escaped without injury, but like all fishermen told his story to others and was advised that the alligator was in the act of laying her eggs and was not scared of anything nor did it intend to be disturbed.

Henry corralled a hunting buddy and one night, armed with a shotgun and flashlight, they bravely paddled a boat out into the river prepared to get that old gator. As the boat drifted down the stream the light caught the big red eyes of the gator swimming silently towards them. Henry's companion held the flashlight with his left hand stretched down the gun barrel and when the gator got within gun range he pulled the trigger. The recoil of the gun kicked the flashlight into the river and suddenly it was dark as pitch. Neither of the hunters have ever told how scared they were, paddling frantically away in the darkness.

The old alligator is now a good sixty years old and has become a sacred legend, enjoying the respect and protection of all the sportsmen near the Alapaha River.

At any rate, most of the natives are convinced the word Alapaha has something to do with alligators.

CHAPTER EIGHT

When only a late teenage boy I became conscious of my good luck to be living in the Thomasville section of our country.

Much of the realization came after my best friend, Vallie Hawthorn, and I, both about the same age, drove a one-horse open rig down the narrow, winding Tallahassee Road in 1905 to Andrew Manning's farm, a distance of eighteen miles. (This farm today is a part of Foshalee Plantation.) It was a long drive without a rest and when our horse became tired and darkness descended we wrapped the lines around the whip stand because we figured the horse could see better than we could. Upon reaching the Foshalee Slough we found that waist-deep water had covered the road, but we finally managed to get across and arrived at the Manning home about ten p. m.—wet, cold and tired.

The Mannings, who kept open house for anyone passing their way, directed a man to take care of our horse and they placed us in a room which we soon learned had homemade wild duck feather mattresses on the beds. When we stretched out to rest our cold weary bodies the comfort of sinking six inches deep and having the warm feathers wrap us up was something we could never forget.

After an early breakfast we left our rig and joined Andrew in his open carriage drawn by two horses, and now we felt mighty important as we proceeded on the journey to Tallahassee. This was an unbelievable trip by today's standards: our two bird dogs hunted on the sides of the road as we traveled along and everytime they pointed we dismounted and shot. All the land was open to shooting, there was no "daily limit," and we were good shots—arriving at our hotel we had three grocery baskets full of quail. Andrew was acquainted with the staff at the girls' college so we dolled up and presented the quail to the college, which act placed us in the good graces of the authorities and gave us the opportunity to meet the small student body. Today this college is nationally known as Florida State University.

Our destination, Panacea on the Gulf of Mexico, was reached about dark the following day and we made arrangements with a guide to take us goose hunting at daybreak.

That was the most bitter cold windy day imaginable, but we bagged one lone goose and started back about dark. The little inboard motor was cranked up and we headed for a dim light on the shore. One moment the light was visible and the next moment it disappeared. Then it dawned on us that the motor had backfired and we were running backwards full speed out to sea.

After making the proper adjustment we arrived safely and laughed all night. What

Lower Cairo Road southwest of Thomasville. Once known as the "Old MacIntyre Road," it is still well traveled and looks about as it did over a hundred years ago.

risk would three young men make for a goose!

It has been over sixty years since one traveled by a horse-drawn vehicle from Thomasville to the Gulf of Mexico. Today when a person in South Georgia seeks a haven of rest and peace he can reach Alligator Point or Panacea in one and a half hours.

Many of the fifty-two doctors composing the staff of the John D. Archbold Memorial Hospital, along with other professional and businessmen, periodically spend a weekend in their own cottages on the Gulf. Others simply haul a motorboat on a trailer behind their car to a convenient launching point on the Gulf.

Few endeavors are more relaxing and stimulating than casually trolling a net and periodically stopping to dump the catch in the bottom of the boat while all aboard scramble to catch the little fish to put them back into the water while keeping the shrimp. The anticipation of fresh shrimp with a pot of hot grits and butter makes the trolling more zestful.

Another great sport is to sight a school of mullet, motor within a few feet of the mass of fish and drift along, casting a weighted hook and with a jerk hooking a fish on every other cast or so. Very few fish in the Gulf are better to eat than fresh mullet, especially when they are with roe. Professional fishermen stay on the lookout for schools of mullet during the fall season. A trained fisherman can arrange a net on the back of a small boat, circle a school of mullet at full speed as his net plays out into the water, then make a smaller circle within the large one and continue this maneuver until he captures just about the entire school.

Among many others, Dr. C. H. Watt, Jr., and his wife, Julie, have a beach home at Alligator Point. When the pressure of his profession becomes too great they go to the Gulf for a day or two, where the sun and fresh air soon invigorates them as they watch for strange or rare birds.

On many weekends my son, R. C. Balfour, III, goes to his summer cottage at Panacea near the mouth of the Ochlocknee River, where his favorite way of spending time is fishing beyond the sight of land.

Each family who enjoys the Gulf seems to have a special reason for seeking such a restful environment where the seafood is delicious and plentiful and the salt air so invigorating.

The early history of Tallahassee, Florida, Thomasville, Georgia, and the area between these two towns helps to explain how this section became molded into one of the most attractive parts of the south.

Acquiring an abstract of title dating back to a Spanish Land Grant made me realize that Florida was a possession of Spain for 300 years except for the short English occupation of 1763-1783. It is true that the Spanish did very little to develop Florida during their long stay. During his reign, King Philip III became discouraged and threatened to abandon St. Augustine because he considered the territory a worthless expense. But the King was sharply reminded that he held Florida by permission of the Pope, with the provision that he make an attempt to bring the Indians to God.

Therefore, Franciscan Fathers were sent to St. Augustine and a chain of missions built every twenty miles along the old Indian trail to the west. Each priest was alone and in complete control, administering to many Christianized Indian families who became devout enough to drop what they were doing at the sound of the chapel bell and gather for worship. They filled the little churches to overflowing, humbly kneeling, making the sign of the cross and worshiping in their own way.

The Indians supported the missions with their labor and love, bringing in game to eat and the skins of deer and bear to sleep on. By 1650 there were more than fifty missions.

During the Spanish rule of Florida there were two capitals, St. Augustine and Pensacola. Therefore, most of the activity or development occurred in these two towns or the territory between them.

The Spanish rule of Florida ended July 15th, 1821, and the American flag was raised at Pensacola in a ceremony attended by General Andrew Jackson and the Spanish Governor of West Florida, Callova. About a year and a half was required to replace the military government of Florida with the civil. General Andrew Jackson resigned as military governor, and the President of the United States, James Monroe, appointed Judge William P. Duval the civil governor of Florida, which office he held from 1823 to 1834.

One of Governor Duval's first official acts was the appointment of John Lee Williams of Pensacola and William H. Simmons of St. Augustine to study the country between the Suwannee and Ochlocknee Rivers for a suitable place to locate a new capital. These two men met at St. Marks and rode horseback for many miles, making a thorough study before selecting an elevated tract of land just south of the deserted fields of Old Tallahassee, which was about halfway between St. Augustine and Pensacola. Congress approved the location and donated a quarter section of land for the town and permitting the quarter section adjoining to be sold to provide money for public buildings. "This initiated the first survey of land in Florida and consequently the capital became the point of intersection of the principal meridian and the first base line."

The name of Tallahassee, a derivation from the Seminole dialect meaning "Suntown" or "Chieftown," was retained. A loghouse was built, where an official council met for the first time in November of 1823, and Tallahassee was declared the permanent capital by the territory's American settlers.

It is said that many years before this location was chosen as the capital, DeSoto and a Spanish expedition spent a full winter in the vicinity. That incident has led to an assumption that the first observance of Christmas in the present United States was conducted in or near this site.

Tallahassee, occupying a spot in the beautiful red hills of Leon County, is surrounded by Lake Jackson, Lake Iamonia, Lake Miccosukee and several smaller lakes. These provide natural habitats for thousands of wild ducks during the winter hunting season and great fresh water fishing in the summer.

We may better understand Governor Duval's background, his self-sufficient disposition and determination from a story told about him. As a young man his father ordered him to bring in a large log for the fireplace, which he claimed was too heavy to carry. His father commanded him not to return to the house until he brought the log.

Young Duval did not return to the house but crossed the mountains into Kentucky, where he educated himself, studied law and was elected to Congress. Many years later he returned to his old home, arriving about the same time of day that he had left, and saw his father and stepmother sitting by the fire. At the wood pile was a log about the same size as the one he was ordered to bring in when a boy, twenty years before. With grim humor he picked it up, went into the house and nonchalantly remarked, "Dad, I have brought the log." The old man glanced up at him and just as nonchalantly replied, "You have been a mighty long time bringing it. Put it on the fire."

It is recorded that Governor Duval "persuaded" the Indians to move down along the Apalachicola and leave their fertile land to the white people. The Indians did not understand the ways of the white American settlers and were far from happy about going.

The Indians better understood the Spanish who were interested in teaching them Christianity and trying to save their souls; also, the British who looked upon them as potential customers. Now the Americans considered them a burden obstructing their progress. "Andrew Jackson said that it was absurd to consider that the Indians had any rights at all."

Many Federal officials felt uneasy about the landgrabs and asked that some legal form be observed. All the chiefs and subchiefs were ordered by Governor Duval to meet at Moultrie Creek and sign a treaty in 1823. The most important chiefs refused to come. Soldiers with drawn bayonets guarded the grounds. The 150 subchiefs and warriors attending were suspicious and out of humor as a few illiterate English speaking Indian-Negroes endeavored to explain the legally intricate language of the treaty. Only a few of the subchiefs made their crossmark on the document. Commissioner Gadsden who was present with the Governor wrote Secretary-of-War Calhoun, "It is not necessary to disguise the fact that the treaty was in a degree a treaty of imposition."

It is difficult today to believe the cruelty which reduced the proud Indians to rags and forced them to beg on the streets while their children starved. Historians tell us that the Christianity taught by the Spanish Priests for three centuries inspired the older Indians to influence their young men, by force if necessary, to seek peace by negotiation. If we had shown more compassion and brought about a better understanding, the Indians could have enjoyed this land with us and America may have been stronger than it is today.

Tallahassee was incorporated in 1825 and became the State Capital when Florida entered the union in 1845.

To begin with Tallahassee was a wild frontier town, but during 1826 the cornerstone was laid for a new capitol building and many houses were built on the newly cut streets given the names of Monroe, Calhoun, Adams and Jefferson. Because of the great demand for cotton, sophisticated planters from Georgia, the Carolinas and Virginia began leaving their worn-out land and moving to the rich, red soil of the Tallahassee area.

Many came by boat to the newly improved port of St. Marks, bringing their families,

mahogany furniture, silver and fine china and living in big comfortable log cabins. There was a great supply of game, wild turkeys, quail, ducks, venison and fish from the gulf and lakes, all of which their Negro cooks prepared to a queen's taste.

Governor Duval recognized the cultural influence of the new planters and moved his family to the capital. Tallahassee was on the way to becoming the historical and beautiful city that it is today.

Napoleon Bonaparte's nephew, Count Achille Murat, set up a large plantation which he named "Lipona" for his native Napoli. Some other plantations were Thomas Randall's "Belmont," Nuttal's "El Destino," White's "Casa Bianca," John Gamble's "Waukeena." Francis Eppes, grandson of Thomas Jefferson, and many more nationally known men created plantations and were destined to influence and direct the future of this area.

General Zachary Taylor won the last large Indian battle in a hammock near the Kissimmee River. The Indians who escaped disappeared into the Everglades, and the others throughout the state who could be caught were rounded up and shipped west.

Many attempts have been made to move the capital of Florida to a more central location because Tallahassee is only a few miles from the Georgia boundary line, but so far it remains where Governor Duval placed it.

The early settlers were men and women of culture and wealth whose influence created a town worthy to be called the capital of Florida. Even with the fast growth of Florida the capital has kept abreast by erecting many beautiful and useful state buildings, while the city has developed two large colleges and other enterprises in keeping with a town representing the government of this wonderful state.

Thomasville, Georgia, is located twelve miles north of the Florida boundary line and thirty-six miles from Tallahassee, the capital of the Sunshine State.

The history of Tallahassee had a great influence on Thomasville. The fifty Spanish missions built every twenty miles commencing at St. Augustine covered a distance of 1,000 miles. A portion of the Spanish Trail meandered across the Florida boundary line south of the present day location of Valdosta and continued through Thomas County Georgia, before re-entering Florida. It is highly possible this loop through Georgia was made without realizing where the Florida line was located. However, it gave the Spanish undisputed possession of the land in southwest Georgia as far back as 1700.

James Oglethorpe founded Savannah in 1733 and through this settlement the colony of Georgia was established. Even so, Spain continued to retain southwest Georgia until the Treaty of Paris in 1763 ended the French and Indian War. This gave England title to Georgia with the exception of southwest Georgia which was now controlled by the Governor of South Carolina who acted under the original Carolina Grant giving him full authority. Only after the American Revolution did South Carolina drop her claim and then southwest Georgia legally became a part of the State of Georgia.

Around 1800 vast numbers of Creek Indians inhabited the Panhandle section of Florida. The Spanish authorities encouraged them to cross the border and attack frontier settlements in Georgia, then retreat, using the State of Florida as protection and a hiding place. These raids prompted the men in Georgia to organize and make several expeditions into Florida without the approval of the U. S. Government, but their efforts failed to accomplish the desired relief. Therefore, when the War of 1812 began, Georgians were fighting Creek Indians instead of British Soldiers.

The Indian Chiefs were wise men who realized if they retained possession of their land it would take the united effort of all the tribes under one leadership and the Shawnee, Creeks and Seminoles tried to form an Indian confederacy but this movement only partly succeeded as the Lower Creeks of Georgia refused to join up. In August, 1813, the Alabama Creeks attacked Fort Mims where settlers from surrounding country had taken refuge and 536 women, children and men were killed with all the soldiers.

Andrew Jackson defeated the Indians in March, 1814, and the Creeks were forced to sign the Treaty of Fort Jackson, thereby relinquishing the rights to most of their land in Alabama and a strip of land sixty miles wide in southern Georgia on the Florida boundary line. According to William Warren Rogers' recent history of Thomas County the land the Indians were allowed to keep in south Georgia was considered worthless. He states, "A Thomas County historian has pointed out that the area was so ill-regarded that certain Georgia legislators opposed improving the region because they did not like spending the state's money trying to develop a country which God Almighty had left in an unfinished condition."

The land was described as "dotted with pine barrens and wiregrass, not considered to have much agriculture potential." The country which became Thomas County was sparsely inhabited by people, "establishing their crude homes, and there lived for generations and generations in unprogressive simplicity and strange isolation."

Most homes were one-room log houses with a clay fireplace and a chimney built of crossed rived strips or slats to hold the soft clay together until a slow fire cured the mud which became as hard as bricks. The small clearings in the woods were used for gardens, and the usual possessions were a mule, a plow and a rifle, as the territory abounded in all kinds of game which was used to feed the families.

A section of the Twelve-Mile Post Road south of Thomasville near the Florida border. This ante-bellum road was used to haul cotton from the fertile fields of South Georgia to Florida ports in wagons drawn by four and sometimes six mules.

CHAPTER NINE

Southwest Georgia, Thomas County and Thomasville participated in the boom in land values when the demand for cotton soared. First there was a great influx of small farmers without slaves, seeking new cheap land where they could work, save and get a start with their families. Later those classified as planters came and acquired large acreages which they cleared and cultivated.

By 1834 there were 60,000 bales of cotton produced in southwest Georgia and north Florida. General Call organized a company which built a railroad, the third line in the United States, to haul cotton from Tallahassee to the boats at St. Marks.

The line was built of light iron and wood and the labor was mostly slave, along with a few half-breed Indians. Mules driven in tandem drew the cars along the road. The passenger coaches were shaped like a box with a row of benches on each side holding eight people. In 1837 a steam locomotive was secured and the hauling capacity increased.

In his 1878 diary, Col. James L. Seward wrote about the formation of Thomas County and founding of the city of Thomasville. The entries were printed verbatim in the Thomasville Press during 1930.

By an act of the Legislature of Georgia, approved 23rd December, 1825, the organization of Thomas County (named for Gen. Jett Thomas), was provided for. The proposition to form a new county entered into the contest for a seat in the Legislature, the candidates being Mag. Harden, who resided on the Chattahoochee, and Capt. T. J. Johnson, who lived six miles south of the present location of Thomasville on the Duncanville Road. (This plantation is now owned by Mrs. Parker Poe and is known as Pebble Hill.) The candidates were both living in Early County as originally formed. Capt. Johnson was the successful candidate. After the act was passed providing for the new county of Thomas, he purchased Land Lot No. 39 in the 13th District of then Irvin County and had it conveyed to the Inferior Court. Aaron Everett, Esq., was commissioned to lay off and survey a courthouse square.

By 1827 the town had made little improvement. A courthouse built of pine logs, roughly split, covered with pine boards and floored with puncheons, roughly braced, constituted the temple of justice.

In November of that year Superior Court was held, with Judge Fort presiding. At that term three Indians were tried for murder of a man by the name of Parish and found guilty and sentenced to be hanged. Judge Fort in pronouncing the death sentence remarked that he would omit the usual benediction as the Indians would not understand it. They were executed in the middle of what is now Broad Street where the Confederate Monument was later placed.

During the period when the Indians were defeated in our section and shipped to Government reservations, only those who had intermarried with the white or black races were left, along with a few who escaped the roundup.

Thomasville's original courthouse was replaced with a beautiful brick building designed by architect John Wind in 1858, by which time the little village was showing definite signs of becoming a substantial town.

Many educated planters living in comfortable ante-bellum homes, owning many slaves, producing a bale of seed cotton to the acre, had established large plantations between Tallahassee and Thomasville from 1837-1865 and "cotton was king." Most of the able-bodied young men were in the Confederate Army when the Civil War came to an end and the slaves freed. So it is easy to imagine the confusion and bedlam that existed. Today the government would rehabilitate a stricken land, but just the reverse occurred then—the Federal Government confiscated all the cotton in the South, the only liquid asset available.

Slavery for the Negroes was deplorable and inhuman, so too for white people was the period of reconstruction with its unjust laws and punishments enforced by "carpet-baggers" and armed soldiers.

Many slaves continued working under a written contract with their former plantation owners who guaranteed their rations, a house to live in and a share of the harvest which amounted to $25 to $100. Other slaves in the Tallahassee, Thomasville area migrated to Jacksonville, Florida, and many nearby large towns.

The well educated planters of culture and wealth not only lost their battle of the Civil War but also lost their battle with the Mexican cotton boll weevil about 1916 and now they were facing a financial battle trying to save their plantations. The substantial planters

realized it was impossible to raise cotton on a large scale and began diversifying their crops. This was an experiment but undoubtedly a step in the right direction. Then followed a program of intensifying the work on small acreages, applying more fertilizer to increase the yield. It was a long period of trial and failure for those who continued to dig a living out of the ground, and the going was rough.

However, something occurred to change the entire outlook for the people of Thomasville and surrounding country. Sir William Osler, for many years a teacher of internal medicine at John Hopkins, in his famous medical textbook named the best climates for tuberculosis as Phoenix, Arizona; Saranac Lake, New York; and Thomasville, Georgia.

The winter climate of Thomasville was much more pleasant than the other places suggested, so Thomasville developed rapidly. First, the boarding houses were filled with visitors who came for their health and sat in Paradise Park breathing the pure air from the pine tree area which seemed to be beneficial. Then the visitors discovered that the abandoned cotton fields were full of Bob White quail, and wealthy and prominent persons the nation over poured in to enjoy the hunting.

Large hotels were built. The first was the Piney Woods which opened December 1st, 1885. It was in the Queen Anne style of architecture, constructed of wood, three stories high with turrets or towers extending a hundred feet in the air. There were several hundred feet of verandas, spacious parlors and a ballroom for entertaining, suites of rooms, private baths and steam heat. These luxuries were almost beyond the dreams of elegant living.

Another hotel built in Thomasville was the Mitchell House, constructed of brick and occupying an entire block in the business section. The front was opposite the Court House and faced a big park with walkways leading to a fountain in the center. This park was

66

enclosed with a white picket fence, making it more private and protecting it from the roaming cows which were allowed to go wherever they liked. A portion of the Mitchell House on Broad Street still remains.

The Masury Hotel was the third largest hotel built for winter tourists and was located

The Stuart House was the fourth hotel erected for the tourists and was located on Madison Street and built of wood.

These hotels became world-renowned and made Thomasville famous as a winter resort, attracting many prominent people from all parts of the United States and abroad. Just

The Piney Woods Hotel, the largest and most elaborate of the several resort hotels in early Thomasville.

at the corner of Broad and Jefferson Streets. It was constructed of brick and the front porch was made of wood, artistically patterned. The Masury Hotel was eventually torn down and this location is now occupied by the Downtown Motor Inn and J. C. Penney Company.

how the wealthiest people in our nation were entertained by these grand hotels located in Thomasville, only eighteen or twenty years after the Civil War, has always intrigued many. There were no automobiles, radios, televisions or Chamber of Commerce organizations—still the guests found wholesome

67

recreation.

Many livery stables furnished saddle horses, surreys with the fringe on top, Victoria carriages, and other rigs, with or without drivers, to see the beautiful virgin forests bordering Pine Tree Boulevard. This boulevard circled Thomasville two miles from the court house and remains today as one of the natural unspoiled scenes in Georgia.

Bicycle races were run on a winding dirt track circling Paradise Park. The contestants rode old-time bicycles having a large wheel about five feet high connected with a small one trailing along in the rear. The riders sat five or six feet in the air and it required great skill to keep perfect balance. The modern bicycles of today were just coming into use and many guests rode them for pleasure.

The wealthy visitors attracted the best entertainment of that period. Sousa's Band gave many concerts and William "Buffalo Bill" Cody brought his Wild West Circus to town with real Indians riding bareback horses. Also,

Annie Oakley and Buffalo Bill displayed their great marksmanship.

When Mr. Rockefeller visited the Piney Woods Hotel he always had a pocketful of new silver dimes and tipped every one he came in contact with ten cents. However, local gossip insisted when he attended services at the Baptist Church he gave $1000.00.

Among Thomasville's early visitors was J. Wyman Jones of Englewood, New Jersey, who purchased between 250 and 300 acres of land on the edge of the city limits from J. S. Seward. Mr. Jones fenced this tract of land and called it Glen Arven Park in honor of his wife who was an Arven. At first Glen Arven was operated as a park with winding drives through the beautiful wooded area. A small portion containing wild deer in a wire enclosure twelve feet high was a special feature. Here rattlesnakes with their fangs removed were placed amongst the deer and guests watched these wild animals pounce on the snakes with their sharp hoofs and cut

The gate at the entrance of Glen Arven
was artistically built in a rustic manner out
of small cypress.

them to pieces.

Golf was being introduced into America about 1890 and Mr. Jones, with a group of friends, organized The Country Club of Thomasville and built a nine hole sand green golf course on Mr. Jones' property. There were forty-eight nationally known visitors and eighteen local men, a total of sixty-six members. The board of governors were: C. M. Chapin, J. Wyman Jones, Charles S. Hebard, S. J. Drake, B. E. Schurneir and Mr. Metcalf, who acted as the first president.

Glen Arven golf course was allowed to grow up in the summer and placed back into playing condition in the winter. It was also a private club and in order for the townspeople to play golf the year around a local golf course was built where the Thomasville High School now stands. This is a picture of a foursome playing on the town golf course, and shows the simple little clubhouse with Doctor Harry Ainsworth's automobile, one of the first cars to appear in Thomasville.

Glen Arven Country Club property was put up for sale in 1910 and a group of northern visitors formed the Glen Arven Land Company, Incorporated, sold stock and purchased the property. The stock is now held by the Cherokee Foundation.

Under the leadership of Rhydon Mays a group of local men leased Glen Arven Country Club and a board of directors has successfully operated the club until this day.

While many have assisted in the welfare of Glen Arven Country Club, the five men who should never be forgotten are J. Wyman Jones, Charles M. Chapin, Howard Hanna, John F. Archbold and J. H. (Jock) Whitney.

Mr. Chapin, Mr. Hanna and Mr. Archbold, with other members of the Land Company, agreed to modernize the nine hole golf course. Styles & Van Kleek of Boston, Massachusetts, and St. Petersburg, Florida, a firm of golf course landscape architects, were commissioned and made an estimate for an eighteen hole grass greens complete layout

This picture shows a section of the first clubhouse which was built at Glen Arven in 1895 and stood for forty-three years before being destroyed by fire on May 30th, 1938.

A typical scene of the early social life of the members on the porch of the wooden clubhouse.

Putting on the original golf course sand greens.

for $75,000.00. Glen Arven Land Company raised $63,000.00 and local members $12,000.00. Work began April 11th, 1929, and required nine months to construct. The course opened for play on February 1st, 1930. However, to the sorrow of all, Mr. Archbold did not live to see it completed.

The course was constructed with mules and hand labor. After the deaths of Mr. Archbold and Mr. Chapin, Howard Hanna sponsored and backed Glen Arven Country Club and always came to the club's rescue in critical times. He also built a magnificent swimming pool at Glen Arven as a memorial to his son, Melville.

John Hay Whitney has always shown a great interest in the welfare of Glen Arven and is responsible for the fairway sprinkler system.

The Glen Arven members have always been proud of their three U. S. Amateur Golf Championship winners, who added much prestige to the club.

Miss Beatrice Hoyt won the championship

A classic picture of W. F. (Bill) MacIntryre after slamming out a mighty drive.

three years in succession, 1896—1897—1898. The picture shown here of Miss Hoyt, attired in a dress of that date, shows the excellent golf form of her back swing.

Miss Frances Griscom was a grand woman claimed by both Thomasville and Tallahassee. How helpful she was to the entire area! Miss Frances died during 1973 at the age of 93.

Miss Mary Lena Faulk began playing golf at an early age on her home course, Glen Arven. Her natural talent became evident as soon she was beating the best players in the club. John Walters, the able golf pro, realized Mary Lena's potential and carefully instructed and advised her.

Mary Lena won the Women's U. S. Amateur Golf Championship in 1953. It is interesting to note that Miss Frances Griscom was present on this occasion, encouraging her on to victory.

The citizens of Thomasville honored Mary Lena with a victory celebration, "the like of which has never been known in Thomasville." After that she visited us in Highlands, North Carolina. I will never forget playing as her partner on the Highlands Country Club course. We were one down going to the 18th

Miss Frances Griscom, one of the area's golfing greats.

72

Mary Lena Faulk putting a ball into the cup on the No. 8 green at Glen Arven.

The author and John Walters on the practice green at Glen Arven. Walters, the golf pro at Glen Arven, was Mary Lena's teacher in her early golfing years.

Miss Hoyt congratulating Mary Lena on winning the 1953 Women's U. S. Amateur Championship.

hole, which demands a good carry over a lake, and her drive was within two inches of the hole—unbelievable!

Mary Lena's main interest in life is golf and she became a professional, playing on the circuit and winning often. She also became a representative of the Spalding Company.

Eddie McElligott, first Golf Pro at Glen Arven.

74

The 16th par three hole which Bobby Jones played with a six iron. Glen Arven Golf Course was carved out of a three hundred acre tract of virgin land, just as the Indians left it. The fairways are lined with many species of pine and hardwood (some as much as 250 years old) which create a unique and pleasing outlook for golfers.

The dog-leg 18th par five hole looking toward the clubhouse of Glen Arven Golf Course. It shows the native dogwood trees in full bloom and the steep terrain of the fairway on the opposite side of a meandering creek which catches many errant shots.

CHAPTER TEN

Nearly all of the guests of the large hotels were eager to hunt quail but this was one sport the management failed to provide, nor did they have know-how to do so. Luckily, many of the men in Thomasville kept a pointer or setter dog to watch their premises and to hunt with during the game season. These men, usually without compensation, began taking the winter visitors hunting on the surrounding open shooting land.

This was a modest beginning but the visitors soon learned that the fields and woodlands abounded with quail. It is recorded that a good shot, hunting on foot with one dog, often bagged thirty or forty quail a day. There was no legal limit and quail were sold by the markets for ten cents each and served by the hotels as a regular diet.

An old picture of early Thomasville's Broad Street. Reportedly, Dr. MacIntosh ran his first automobile into the fence around the Confederate Monument, yelling "Whoa, dammit, whoa!"

Within a few years the winter hotels made an all-out effort to supply their guests with guides, dogs and conveyances to reach their hunting grounds. Many acres of land were leased for hunting and posted signs warning the public against trespassing appeared for the first time in South Georgia.

It is estimated there were eight thousand visitors in Thomasville during the winter of 1887-88 and the town was doing a booming business. Smart, expensive shops were opened and real estate purchases were frequent.

Greenwood Plantation was bought by S. R.

Screven County. Both sides of the family owned the land.

Mr. and Mrs. Jones moved to Thomas County in 1827 and built a frame house which they used as a temporary home until the brick house which still stands was constructed. This magnificent edifice required nine years to build and was a tremendous undertaking.

John Wind, an English architect and graduate of Queen's School for Fine Workmanship, whose diploma carried the signature of Queen Victoria, drew the plans. Brickmakers burned the brick in kilns on the place.

VanDuzer of New York in 1889. This grand old plantation, located only two miles west of Thomasville, depicts the early history of this area. The land was first inherited by Thomas Jones of Bullock County, Georgia, and his 17 year old wife, Lavinia Young of

Lime and cement came by boat to St. Marks, Florida, and Newport, Florida, and from there was hauled by wagon. Sand was taken from the Ochlocknee River, the heavy framing was hewn from the longleaf pine trees on the place. With a pocket knife Mr. Wind chipped and cut out the beautiful frescoes above the columns on the front of the house.

John Wind, the father of the editor of the Cairo Messenger, deserves great credit for the successful completion of this noble home which stands so majestically today.

Following Mr. Jones's death, his wife sold Greenwood on April 24th, 1889, to Mr. VanDuzer. Ten years later, Melville Hanna from Cleveland, a brother of Senator Mark Hanna, persuaded Col. Oliver H. Payne of New York to buy Greenwood and upon Colonel Payne's death it became the property of his nephew, Payne Whitney. Mrs. Helen Hay Whitney inherited the property from her husband. It has since been passed on to their son J. H. (Jock) Whitney, who was ambassador to England and well-known in the financial world. Jock Whitney, as his friends in Thomasville call him, is deeply attached to Greenwood. He is preserving the fine buildings and carrying on the tradition that has existed for so long.

Often little incidents give an insight into a man's character, what he stands for, how he thinks, etc. Recently Patrick Fenlon, Director of Archbold Hospital, and I were playing Mr. Whitney and his guest a round of golf at Glen Arven and after driving, Jock asked what we were playing for and I said,

One of the winding roads on the old Masury place, Myrtlewood Plantation.

78

"The Hall," first bought by Col. Lew Thompson and later owned by Herbert L. Stoddard.

"Fifty-cents Nassau."

Mr. Whitney won only one dollar and a half. However, he said, "That was an enjoyable game and we played hard to win. Golf is too fine a game to spoil by high stakes and it was refreshing to play for fifty-cents Nassau."

In 1888 John W. Masury of New York bought a sizable tract of land near the city limits of Thomasville and erected a large home. This plantation was known as Cleveland Park and is now owned by Balfour Land Company. Mr. Masury, a nationally known paint manufacturer, also built the Masury Hotel in Thomasville.

During the last century many outstanding sportsmen have visited or owned plantations in the Thomasville-Tallahassee area. But, without a doubt, Colonel Lew S. Thompson of Red Bank, New Jersey, and owner of Sunny Hill Plantation, was the greatest field shot of them all.

Like all good sportsmen of his day he shot a double barrel gun and often killed two ducks from a flight reloaded with shells palmed in his hand and bagged two more before they could get out of range.

His famous father was William P. Thompson, an officer in the Confederate Army, who later founded the National Lead Company which merged with John D. Rockefeller's Standard Oil Trust. William P. Thompson became one of the early top executives in that company.

A story was circulated that his son invested in Standard Oil stock and became independently wealthy. He never pretended to work but spent his time in the outdoors hunting, and got to be one of the best marksmen in America. He was commissioned a Colonel by the U. S. Government during World War One when he purchased three seaplanes and trained the pilots, giving the 'planes and his time to his country. Col. Thompson came to Thomasville in the fall of 1905 to find out if the quail shooting was as fabulous as his friend, Edward Crozier, had pictured it.

He brought his servants and temporarily camped in two tents. This gave him an opportunity to discover the bountiful wild game resources of the land between Thomasville and Tallahassee. He soon purchased the hunting lease held by Mr. Crozier and acquired "The Hall," a hunting camp on the Meridian Road owned by Judge W. H. Hopkins and consisting of several hundred acres.

Within a few years he purchased the former home, land and small store of William Ponder known as Sunny Hill. He continued adding many small and large farms, eventually amassing twenty thousand acres.

Robert E. Stringer, a highly respected and capable farmer who owned 1,500 acres of land located near Sunny Hill, was employed as Lew Thompson's manager and held the position for thirty-five years. Mr. and Mrs. Stringer's family consisted of three boys and two girls, Robert E. Stringer, Jr., Sidney H. Stringer, Albert L. Stringer, Ruth and Mary Stringer. The three boys loved the outdoor life and had every opportunity to observe and learn about game, because the entire aim and purpose of Sunny Hill Plantation was to provide better shooting territory and more game.

Young Robert Stringer learned to handle the bird dogs and gave Col. Lew Thompson ten years of his service before going with H. P. Davison, a member of J. P. Morgan Co., bankers of New York City, who owned Springwood Plantation. Later Percy Chubb purchased this beautiful property on the

Thomasville-Tallahassee Road and Robert continued his connection with Springwood for forty years.

The owners of the large plantations did not restrict themselves or their guests to a daily limit until they realized there was a growing shortage of quail. The fact prompted Col. Thompson and a group of his friends to contact the U. S. Biological Survey, at Washington, D. C., during 1923. They requested the best man available for the purpose of making a study of the quail with a view toward increasing the dwindling supply.

Herbert L. Stoddard, connected with the Field Museum in Chicago, Illinois, arrived and made the survey which was very successful. He was a careful scientist and a dedicated naturalist, working with quail probably longer and with better results than any man known. His books on this subject are accepted with thanks and appreciation by all hunters. During much of his research he lived in "The Hall" and Sidney Stringer worked alongside him, living in the same house. Sidney developed into a game expert, later working for Charles Chapin and still later for Dr. and Mrs. Krech.

After Mr. Stoddard finished his first study of the quail situation and was leaving for his home, he remarked to Sidney that he would like to retire in this area some day and for Sid to be on the lookout for a place. Sidney mentioned this to Mr. Thompson and he gave Mr. Stoddard "The Hall," and several hundred acres of fine timber land. It was a wonderful gift, and was Mr. Thompson's way of showing his appreciation to a noted ornithologist who lived in our midst and improved the game management for the benefit of all.

Albert Stringer worked as assistant manager of Sunny Hill under his father and later assumed the full managerial duties, working in this capacity for fifteen years. During this period Sunny Hill was sold to Walter Edge and Albert continued to manage and develop this noted plantation.

Albert Stringer had a standing date every

morning before day during the duck season to motor Col. Thompson to Lake Iamonia. When they arrived, Jerry Nash, a highly respected Negro boatman and a splendid citizen, met Col. Thompson and acted as guide. One day as Albert and the Colonel were driving back to Sunny Hill, after a most exciting and successful hunt, the Colonel said, "Albert, wait a second. You see that woman sitting by the little water hole—she is there every morning. I want to speak to her."

The Colonel said, "Auntie, every morning I notice you sitting here by this little water hole fishing. Do you ever catch anything?" The woman never changed expression but replied, "Naw sir." "Well, why do you continue to fish here?" She smiled and replied, "Because it's so handy." The incident illustrates how slowly life moved in the greatest quail country in America at the turn of the century.

Col. Thompson was a large, handsome man who brought much joy into the lives of many people, assisting those in distress and usually investigating their needs in person. He married Geraldine Morgan in 1895 and their winters were spent at Sunny Hill until his death in 1936.

Geraldine Thompson, who died at the age of 95 in 1967, was a noted humanitarian and philanthropist. It was written that ". . . she had a great love of nature and desired to conserve it. In 1954 she founded the Natural Science Center for young people at the Museum of Natural History in New York City. Both her appreciation of nature and her sense of responsibility and public service were passed on to her granddaughter, Mrs. Post."

Mrs. Post recalls spending many Christmases at Sunny Hill before Col. Thompson's death and later visiting Ed Komarek for a year at his home, "Birdsong."

Mr. and Mrs. Komarek are both nature students. I have several times heard my daughter, Mrs. Bolling Jones, III, and Dr. and Mrs. C. H. Watt, Jr., three of the most enthusiastic bird watchers in Thomasville,

talk about Birdsong and the great number of different species of birds the Komareks have attracted to their bird sanctuary.

Mr. and Mrs. Komarek have a thorough knowledge of the local birds as well as the migratory ones which pay them a visit in the fall and spring. This makes Birdsong doubly attractive to many people in this section.

Quoting an article by Lucy Bullard in the Tallahassee Democrat of October 20th, 1968, "Sunday, October 20, 1968, a dedication ceremony formally marked the refurnishing and reequipment of the Udo Fleichman Natural Science Building at Tallahassee Junior Museum. This work was made possible by the Geraldine Thompson Memorial Fund established by Peggy Post to the memory of her grandmother and augmented by a gift from Mrs. John Lloyd Butler of Saticay, California, mother of Mrs. Post and daughter-in-law of Mrs. Thompson."

The information handed down by word of mouth leads one to believe that the influence of Col. Lewis S. Thompson of Sunny Hill was also a great factor in the decision of many prominent families to locate in this area.

It is impossible to write about all the distinguished people and their plantations in this area, but some day a book should record in detail their importance here and in America.

The grand old hotels of Thomasville played a prominent part in the early history of Thomas County because they attracted so many visitors who became acquainted with the climate, game resources and natural recreational surroundings. The hotels brought Thomasville prosperity and were a financial blessing from 1885 until the turn of the century. Then the winter tourists began flocking to Florida and it became evident that the hotels were destined to close their doors.

The closing of the hotels made for a financial shock and would have been a calamity except for the northerners who had purchased nearby plantations, building winter homes and

Present-day North Dawson Street, Thomasville.

developing game preserves. In the beginning only a few risked buying the very large tracts. However, those early pioneers were so delighted with the results that others soon followed their lead. It is doubtful if any one or two persons could be given the credit for the great number of winter homes and game preserves between Thomasville and Tallahassee. But, it is a fact that Melville Hanna and his brother, Mark Hanna, their descendants, friends and business associates influenced many to acquire plantations.

Senator Mark Hanna did not invest in Thomas County land but rented a home at 830 N. Dawson Street. He once had as his guest Governor William McKinley of Ohio. It was in Thomasville that Governor McKinley's successful presidential campaign was planned. Senator Hanna entertained Governor McKinley at the Mitchell House Hotel, giving a huge reception which was attended by many visitors and local people.

After McKinley was elected president, he and Vice-President Hobart returned to Thomasville for a visit with Senator Mark Hanna. McKinley was the first president after the Civil War to break down sectional feeling and to bring about a new understanding and good will between the North and South.

When President McKinley was shot by the

radical, Leon Czolgosz, Senator Hanna wired his brother Melville in Thomasville requesting that Dr. T. M. McIntosh be rushed to the bedside for consultation with the attending physicians.

After the consultation it was decided an operation was necessary to remove the bullet. Dr. McIntosh disagreed, stating in his opinion the President was unable to stand the operation and perhaps, leaving the bullet, the President could recover as he did not believe it was in a vital place. There were, of course, no drugs in those days to combat infection.

Dr. McIntosh was overruled and the operation performed. Dr. McIntosh was quoted as saying, "Gentlemen, I have done all I can. I am going home." He returned on his special train consisting of an engine and one coach. He could have been right in his decision or wrong. We will never know.

Dr. McIntosh earned a medical degree at the Atlanta Medical College, then attended the Poly Clinic in New York and clinics in Heidelberg, Germany. He was a small man with a definite aim, who made decisions he seldom changed. He was one of the first doctors to cut a person open and remove the appendix. The following story has been handed down for several generations.

One night during 1906 he was called to the bedside of B. F. Herring, our local undertaker, who was in great pain. It was raining and the only mode of transportation available was an open horse drawn wagon, which was impractical to use. Therefore, the ingenious doctor padded the top of a packing box made to store blankets, stretched his patient out on the homemade operating table and performed one of the first successful appendectomies. Mrs. Herring assisted the doctor while another member of the family worked a prism kerosene lamp up and down on a chain so the doctor could see.

This information was furnished by my good friend, Frank Eidson, who got it from Judge Hugh J. MacIntyre, one of Thomasville's outstanding lawyers of that period. It was also approved by Miss Herring.

Quoting Albert Riley in his article, "Pines and Live Oaks, Plantations and Hunting Lodges:"

"Although Mark Hanna never owned a Southern plantation himself, his brother Melville Hanna did, and so did their sisters, Mrs. J. C. Morse and Mrs. C. M. Chapin (who later became Mrs. J. Wyman Jones). Their descendants have carried on the Thomasville plantation tradition. It was through the Hannas that George Humphrey, who had been president of the M. A. Hanna Company before joining Eisenhower's cabinet, became interested in Thomasville.

"There have been perhaps more plantation owners from Cleveland than from any other city, followed by New York. The Hannas and Whitneys influenced many others to buy land in the area. One of the earliest of the plantations was Melrose, owned by Melville Hanna and passed on to his son Howard Hanna, and now owned by the grandchildren, Mrs. Julian Bolton, Mrs. Warren Bicknell and by Mrs. Royal Firman, Jr. Adjoining it is Pebble Hill Plantation, handed down to Mrs. R. L. Ireland, later Mrs. P. W. Harvey, and on to the present owners and descendants, Mrs. Parker Poe and Livingston Ireland. Then there is Springhill owned by Mrs. Ralph Perkins, another of the Hanna clan. Nearby is Elsoma, formerly owned by C. M. Chapin and the late Mrs. Shepherd Krech; and Winstead, the beautiful white columned home formerly owned by the late Coburn Haskell, the man who made the first rubber-cored golf ball, and his wife Gertrude Hanna Haskell. It is now owned by Mr. and Mrs. Philip G. Rust. Another one of the Hanna-family properties is Sinkola Plantation.

"Plantations around Thomasville and Tallahassee are too numerous to list or attempt to describe. But a few in addition to the foregoing should be mentioned. One of the original plantations is Susina, bought in the early days by A. H. Mason of Philadelphia and still owned by his granchildren.

"Springwood is another of the original plantations. Owner Irwin MacIntyre, a Thomasville man, sold to Henry P. Davison, who in turn sold this lovely old home and estate to the late Percy Chubb. It was inherited by his brother, the late Hendon Chubb, then passed on to his son, the late Thomas C. Chubb, an author of distinction, and is now owned by Mrs. Thomas Chubb."

Millpond Plantation was established by Jeptha H. Wade of Cleveland, Ohio, during 1901, and after seventy years it remains one of the most naturally beautiful places in this area. It begins at the south border of the city limits of Thomasville and extends to within a few miles of Metcalf. The Millpond holdings have been divided equally among the Wade heirs, Mrs. Ellery Sedgwick, Jr., J. H. Wade and Mrs. A. Dean Perry. Below are Mr. Wade and Mr. Sholes who have driven out on Millpond Plantation and met their hunting wagon for a day's shooting. Many of the dogs are bobtailed.

My contemporary and friend, the late Garry Wade, often shot quail with me and was so fast with a gun I felt that he was shooting from the hip on a covey rise. At that time I was shooting a 20 gauge automatic gun and although Garry was a wonderful companion he let me know that he was frightened to be around a repeating gun. Therefore, after shooting the next covey rise and returning to the hunting wagon I called his attention to the careful way I unloaded the automatic. I said, "See," and then held up the gun in the air and pulled the trigger. Believe it or not it fired and scared us almost to death. That converted me instantly and I have used a double-barreled gun ever since.

The Norias Hunting Club on Lake Micco-

sukee was organized, to begin with, as a club composed of, among others, the late Walter C. Teagle, head of the Standard Oil Company, the late Senator and Ambassador, W. E. Edge of New Jersey, and Robert W. Woodruff, head of the Coca Cola Company.

The story goes that those who came for quail shooting late in the season became dissatisfied with the scarcity of birds and Walter Teagle became sole owner of the property, naming it Norias Plantation. Senator Edge then purchased Sunny Hill, and Robert W. Woodruff established his own "Ichauway" Plantation between Newton and Albany.

Mr. and Mrs. Teagle spent the winters at Norias Plantation and I became a close friend, often shooting quail with him while Ben Breedlove worked the dogs.

One day I gave Mrs. Teagle a box of selected oranges from a small grove I owned in Winter Haven, Florida. She was so appreciative of this little deed that she always gave me some small token everytime I visited them. She was the only woman I ever saw who had eyes the true, deep color of violets, and they expressed love for everyone she came in contact with.

I persuaded Mr. Teagle and his lifelong friend, James F. Bell of Madreland Plantation, to serve as trustees of the Archbold Hospital and together they persuaded Hendon Chubb of Springwood Plantation to join them. These three men were solely in charge of the endowment fund, amounting to slightly over $300,000.00, and through their efforts while they were serving, the fund grew to the unbelievable sum of slightly over two million dollars.

Again quoting Albert Riley, "One of the early winter residents was the late H. K. Devereaux from Cleveland, who named his plantation Hollywood many years before Hollywood, California, won fame as the movie capital of the world.

"A harness racehorse enthusiast, Sportsman Devereaux maintained a fine stable of trotters and pacers in the winter. They trained on a racetrack at his Pastime Stables inside the city limits.

"Hollywood and the Pastime Stables have been replaced in more recent years by residential subdivisions in and on the south edge of town across from the Glen Arven Country Club. A palatial columned mansion built by the Devereaux family is now locally owned.

"The modern day counterpart to Devereaux and his racehorse training stables is Leonard Buck and his winter quarters for his thoroughbred trotters and pacers at his Allwood Plantation."

The plantation owners always showed an aesthetic interest in the pineywoods and a personal interest in the welfare of the local people. As far back as 1886 Edward Beadel developed Tall Timbers Plantation. Upon his death in 1919 his nephew, Henry Beadel, inherited this beautiful estate which borders Lake Iamonia.

Henry Beadel's great love for this area and interest in wildlife conservation influenced him to make a research station out of his 2,800 acre plantation. In 1958 he established Tall Timbers Research, Inc., dedicated to inde-

The old Beadel home, now Tall Timbers Research Station.

pendent ecological research and administered by a board of directors with a staff of scientists. Henry Beadel served as the first president. Herbert L. Stoddard, Sr. was the second president, followed by Mrs. Parker Poe.

Upon his death in 1963 he left to the institution a considerable endowment which was substantially increased at the death of his brother, Gerald Beadel, who at one time owned about 800 acres of Tall Timbers and was a frequent visitor during the shooting season.

Henry Beadel's unselfish gift, operated as it is today, will be beneficial not only to the woodland owners in this area but to forest and wildlife lands all over America.

John D. Archbold developed Chinquapin Plantation in 1910 and spent the winters there until his death. His son, John F. Archbold, inherited Chinquapin and occupied the lovely plantation with his family. He eventually moved his citizenship to Thomas County and made Thomasville his permanent home. He was a modest, reserved man who felt at home in the Rotary Club with those who called him "Jack." His closest friends were J. B. Jemison, E. R. Jerger, Dr. A. D. Little and W. F. MacIntyre.

Jack Archbold was anxious to set up a fine, living memorial for his late father and considered many projects without finding one he thought suitable. Then he underwent surgery in the old Thomasville City Hospital and realized the need for an up-to-date institution. He at once called in architects and engineers and soon built the John D. Archbold Memorial Hospital, which opened June 20, 1925, for the benefit of all the people in the Thomasville area. He also built a nursing school and home for nurses, "The Annie Mills Archbold School of Nursing," in memory of his mother.

Mr. Archbold went all the way, establishing an endowment fund which assured the continued operation of the hospital. The people of the entire area will remain eternally thankful for this, the greatest gift ever bestowed upon them.

The hospital has grown and expanded until its facilities are now more than double its original size. Recently a Mental Health Center and a Cobalt Therapy Unit were added. At the same time a new emergency room-outpatient department was added, which nearly tripled the size of the previous department. In 1970 the bed complement grew to 200 and a fourth and fifth floor are now being added.

The citizens of Thomasville and Thomas County are always ready to perform any task for their hospital which is supported by income from patients, contributions from municipal and county, and from private individual donors and endowment funds. Patrick I. Fenlon, Vice-President and Director in charge of the overall operation, with a strong board of trustees who serve without compensation, has successfully guided the destiny of the John D. Archbold Memorial Hospital for the past ten years.

There are now fifty-two doctors on the staff representing more than sixteen different medical specialties. The cooperation between the medical staff and the director and trustees has always been one of the goals desired and worked for.

The highlight of the hunting season is the dove shoot the entire staff tries to attend near Faceville, Georgia. There are thirty-three members of the Archbold Memorial Hospital staff in these two pictures, ready to shoot. Has anyone seen this many doctors all smiling at one time?

Well, there is a catch in this too, for Dr. Jim Neill had just captured a rattlesnake with his bare hands and Johnny Jones cut the snake's head off with one swipe of a butcher knife.

The citizens of the Thomasville-Tallahassee community are an easy going, hospitable lot and have enjoyed a fine relationship with the winter residents and plantation owners. Many prominent and influential persons are guests at the plantations, and they come and go without publicity or interference.

The Duke and Duchess of Windsor were guests for many winters of Mrs. George F. Baker at Horseshoe Plantation, located between Tallahassee and Thomasville. The Duke became an honorary member of the Georgia-

Florida Field Trial Club and was invited to shoot quail on several of the other plantations. He proved to be an excellent marksman.

However, when Senator Edge invited the Duke on a wild turkey drive, asking him to be at Sunny Hill Plantation before daybreak, the Duke accepted but was at a loss to know what was going on. Albert Stringer, superintendent of the plantation, managed the hunt. He had a group of farm boys on hand and assigned one to each hunter to carry an empty shell box for the guest to sit on, and he showed the guests to their stands.

It was still dark when Albert ordered a boy to pick up a box and follow him, and after walking a good distance he told him where to put it down. The boy obeyed with nary a word. When day broke Albert saw he had

been commanding the Duke of Windsor and former King of England. He tried to apologize but a whistle had blown—the drive was underway and turkeys were flying. The Duke missed his first shot, then Albert suggested they were flying faster than appeared and to lead them more. Next the Duke tried a right and a left shot, and got both.

After the hunt the Duke insisted on carrying back the box and one of the turkeys, enjoying the joke every bit as much as the other hunters. All the local people who got to know the royal couple remember them as friendly and personable.

While George M. Humphrey was Secretary of the Treasury in President Eisenhower's cabinet the President occasionally visited him at his winter home, Milestone

Guest cottage on Milestone Plantation where President and Mrs. Eisenhower stayed on their visits.

A section of the flower garden at Milestone Plantation.

Plantation, a few miles south of Thomasville.

Relaxing on a rubber-tired hunting wagon equipped with comfortable seats, drawn by two well-groomed mules, with keen interest he would watch Rufus, the dog trainer, handle the pointer and setter dogs from horseback. Then, when Rufus held his red cap high above his head and called out, "Point!" business picked up. The President and Mr. Humphrey lost no time getting their double-barrelled guns and walking briskly up to and past the dogs. Rufus walked between them with whip in hand, flushing the quail. Even old hunters are always startled at the flutter of quail wings as the birds explode from the ground cover, and Mr. Humphrey and the President were no exceptions. They were both good shots and would watch the dogs stand firm to shot and wing as a Brittany Spaniel retrieved the dead birds.

Many times the birds are not moving and even the best dogs cannot find them. Most hunters are aware of this fact and glad to take a breather which gives them time to be aware of God's great creation. The hunting wagon may be skirting the edge of a cornfield or entering a wiregrass section covered with longleaf or slash pine trees, where selective cutting has been practiced for years. This insures a continued stand of timber as the small trees replace the large ones. There is always something of interest in the outdoors for quail hunters to see and discuss.

After a hunter shoots all day from a hunt-

George M. Humphrey, President Dwight Eisenhower and Rufus, the dog handler, just before climbing aboard the hunting wagon for a quail hunt at Milestone. They are shooting twenty gauge double-barreled shotguns and shells loaded with number nine shot. The smiles show their anticipation of a fine outing.

ing wagon, kicks off his rattlesnake-proof boots, takes a refreshing drink and feels the blood tingle through his system and invigorate every fiber of his body he is apt to sit back and in retrospect relive the highlights of the day.

Arnold Palmer, the great golfer, said, "The biggest things in President Eisenhower's life were his family and golf. He loved the game. When he was on the course he could shut out the cares of the world." It was an excellent form of relaxation for him and when visiting Milestone he always managed to get in at least one round of golf on the beautiful Glen Arven course.

That was during a period when President Eisenhower was recovering from a heart attack and golf carts were replacing the vanishing caddies. However, at first there were only two carts. The President used one and the Secret Service men concealed an army rifle in a golf bag and patrolled the golf links with the other.

The eighteenth hole at Glen Arven is a par five uphill fairway. The President tested his strength by walking this steep grade without puffing and the next day announced for re-election.

The morning President Eisenhower was leaving Milestone, everyone connected with the Plantation gathered around to shake his hand as he thanked them. Rufus, the dog trainer, was so overcome he told the President to come back soon for he enjoyed handling him.

George M. Humphrey enjoyed his lovely plantation, and he was very popular locally. One week he might entertain President Eisenhower and the next week speak at the Thomasville Rotary Club.

He was always a shrewd, practical and far-seeing man. Well do I remember him coming into my little office for the first time and offering to purchase the Archbold land from a group of local men who had acquired it. He was direct and named the price he would pay if we re-roofed ten small tenant houses. His offer was made in a pleasant manner and I replied that I would readily make the same offer. We both laughed. After a few more sessions he made a trade to purchase the land in the presence of Dozier Hasty and me and Milestone was on the way to being developed.

The people of South Georgia appreciated the President's visit and were enthusiastic and excited. However, as with all visitors to the area, they had no trouble leaving him alone to enjoy his stay.

There was a saying for many years that the plantation owners "would rather have a covey of quail than to raise a thousand bushels of corn." However, time marched on and conditions changed. One of the first to take a new look was Major L. A. Beard when he became manager of Greenwood. He concluded it was possible to operate the plantation as a business and make a profit while providing even better recreation for the owner. Major Beard studied the results of scientific research by Herbert Stoddard, E. V. Komarek and his brother, Roy Komarek, showing that the quail population is essentially governed by the amount of proper food available and the cover to protect them.

Even though the land owners had learned how to maintain a fair supply of quail, the average yield of corn in Georgia was only about eight bushels per acre.

The following story of hybrid corn was written by Herbert K. Hayes from information made available by W. H. Freeman, with A. A. Fleming furnishing the story of Greenwood Seed Company:

"In 1945 Mr. John Hay Whitney, owner of Greenwood Farms, set aside these holdings to be used for the betterment of Southern agriculture. This was done initially under the supervision of Major L. A. Beard with E. V. and Roy Komarek as managers. And later under Mr. Whitney on the death of Major Beard in 1954.

"The facilities of the plantation were placed at the disposal of the Georgia Coastal Plain Experiment Station. First seed production took place in 1945 with Florida W-1, a white hybrid developed by Fred H. Hull. The acreages were utilized for experimental hybrid production, yield testing, and foundation seed production. *It was through the financing of Greenwood Farms that the foundation seed stock for hybrid seed in Georgia was made available* to growers in the state and in the South.

"In 1948, the Georgia Coastal Plain Experiment Station released Dixie 18, a yellow hybrid, to the Coastal Plain. Greenwood Seed Company expanded production of this hybrid so that at one time the entire production of over 3,500 acres was devoted to this hybrid.

"Since 1953 Greenwood has established a corn breeding program and has developed several hybrids in keeping with one of its primary objectives, the betterment of Southern agriculture."

Since the development of hybrid corn the yield per acre has reached as much as 80 bushels. Nearly all corn is now gathered with a combine which shells the grain, but in the process a small amount is lost on the ground. The quail feed on this during the entire hunting season.

Major Beard's dream is now coming true. The good plantation managers strive to produce an income, using the modern machinery which has largely replaced farm labor, and by practicing up-to-date forestry. All of which has been most rewarding. The more the land is fertilized and worked the better the natural seed develops for birds. Therefore, it is something like "having your cake and eating it too."

The plantations between Thomasville and

Tallahassee have become more and more an asset to our section, always willing to experiment with the most modern ways of farming and entering into the welfare of the area. The men who make them "run" are a fine group—they love their outdoor work and take great pride in it.

As might be expected, these men are wise in the ways of the wild creatures. One of the best authorities, the late Carlton Hunley of Greenwood, made a hobby of catching snakes alive and handling them with his bare hands

George Herring and Sonny Lee, two skilled foresters, display a six-foot-plus rattlesnake—dead but still scary.

years before Ross Allen started his Reptile Institute at Silver Springs, Florida.

Carlton was also something of a prankster. At the time the movie "Bring 'em Back Alive" was at the height of its popularity the renowned big-game hunter, Frank Buck, visited Major Beard at Greenwood. Buck was kind enough to talk to the plantation "hands" and tell them about the perils and problems of filming the wild animals, detailing in particular the highlight of the film, a fight to the finish between a black panther and a boa constrictor snake. Carlton had previously decided, while watching the movie, that practically all the incidents and confrontations were staged and not natural, but he kept his reservations to himself.

Upon learning the next day that the guests were to take a moonlight tour of the gardens after dinner, Carlton placed a huge but thoroughly dead rattlesnake in one of the main walks. His companions were in on the joke and concealed themselves in the bushes. All agreed later that however Spartan brave Frank Buck may have been in Africa, when his feet tangled that night with the rattlesnake his yelling could have been heard a mile away.

Only as far back as 1930 the sawmill operators knew very little about caring for the forests. The custom then was to purchase a timber lease, cut every desirable tree and move away, after which the landowner burned the woods in preparation for cattle grazing. This procedure made it impossible for the seed to sprout and reforest the land.

I always had a desire to conserve and protect our timberlands, but never was able to sell the idea to a sawmill operation. Therefore, in 1937 I established the Balfour Lumber Company for the purpose of practicing "selective cutting" on our own lands and on any of the surrounding plantations whose owners or managers were conservation minded. I knew very little about the manufacturing of lumber—my interest was in the woods where I personally marked with a hatchet only the old ripe trees with flat tops and the larger trees in crowded stands.

Within six months Paul Dunn and Byron Keaton, our woodsmen, caught on to the idea and became as enthusiastic as I was. That was the beginning of the first program of its kind perhaps in the South, certainly within our section.

The first experimental cutting began on Mr. Morse Eley's plantation bordering Pine-tree Boulevard. The second was entrusted to us by Mrs. Helen Hay Whitney of Green-wood. The work on Greenwood came about as a result of an interview Mrs. Whitney gave me one cool winter morning on the porch of her famous ante-bellum home. When I arrived she selected a sunny warm spot and graciously started the conversation by asking why she should allow me to cut her trees. I explained that all trees have a length of life to live, the

same as people. That a little tree will not grow under a big one and we could assist nature by removing the ripe ones and thereby keep her original longleaf forest in a much healthier growing condition.

Our work was done while both owners were away for the summer, and so carefully and neatly done that when they returned for the winter they could not believe trees had been removed. So impressive were these logging jobs that in a short while all foresters and most sawmill operators in the area had adopted the method.

Getting the early start on the practice of selective cutting, I began experimenting with other conservation possibilities and found that it is not only practicable to perpetuate timber stands but to restore them after hardwood scrub has taken over. The following picture

shows how one 3,000-acre tract of hardwood brush and scattered old longleaf pine was transformed into a beautiful young forest. The brush was poisoned, pushed up and burned, then the land was chopped with a brush cutter. The remaining longleaf pines reseeded the area, which is now known as the O'Neal Forest.

Joe Milam, a skillful and experienced man who knows how to use fire in the woods, waited until the seedlings were three years old and burned the land at night. It required fourteen years to accomplish what is shown in this picture. Now the land is productive, highly so.

Incidentally, good quail shooting on tracts such as this can be managed by the use of bird feeders and grain patches. I love to hunt quail but I am a forester and a lumberman, so trees are my first concern.

While cutting timber on Mrs. Parker Poe's Pebble Hill Plantation our woodsmen found an old half-burned and partly buried golf ball which they brought to me. Mrs. Poe stated that the ball came from a location Coburn Haskell used as a driving range when he was developing the rubber-wound golf ball. This intrigued me because I have always been an enthusiastic golfer and knew that Coburn Haskell had something to do with developing the modern golf ball. I had played many rounds of golf at Glen Arven in a foursome with Katherine Haskell Perkins, Mrs. Frances I. Laurie and Bill MacIntyre, but no one talked about the golf ball, not even Katherine, Coburn Haskell's daughter.

I gave the old golf ball to Katherine's husband, Ralph Perkins, and asked him to get me some information to use in a history of Glen Arven Country Club.

Buddy Highsmih (right) watches the author walk in to flush a single quail.

Ralph collected bits from old newspapers in Cleveland, Ohio, and wrote the first article I had ever seen about the Coburn Haskell golf ball. His research showed that the Haskell patent for a rubber cored golf ball was granted in 1899, after which golf rapidly gained in popularity. Players who could not get interested in playing the dead gutta-percha ball found a thrill in the new Haskell ball. Golfers in Cleveland jumped from a few hundred in 1900 to over 50,000 in 1930.

Today there is a grand book by John Stuart Martin, "The Curious History of the Golf Ball, Mankind's Most Fascinating Sphere." This is a book every golfer should read. It depicts the determination of Coburn Haskell to make a rubber-wound ball to make golf a better game. I like to think the old ball our woodsmen found played a vital part in the development of the new ball.

This is a picture of Winstead Plantation, the former winter home of Mr. and Mrs. Coburn Haskell, as it appears today. It was here that Mr. Haskell experimented with the rubber-wound golf ball at the turn of the nineteenth century. Mr. and Mrs. Haskell's four children spent their early life at Winstead. Katherine became Mrs. Ralph Perkins and purchased Springhill Plantation where she continues to reside. Mary married Mr. Hunter and developed Tarva Plantation in the Albany, Georgia, area. Gertrude became Mrs. Brigham Britton and occupies their lovely Fair Oaks Plantation on the Tallahassee Road, a few miles from Thomasville. Melville, the only son, resides in Tucson, Arizona.

Mrs. Ralph Perkins' children, Mr. and Mrs. Leigh Perkins, Mr. and Mrs. George Oliva and Mr. and Mrs. Berry Sullivan now have their own plantations and continue to carry on the family tradition. Quite obviously they all love this area.

Mr. and Mrs. Philip G. Rust purchased Winstead Plantation in 1948 and have added many acres adjoining this lovely historical place. Mr. Rust and his son, Philip, Jr., have

developed one of the outstanding herds of purebred Santa Gertrudis cattle in the south.

The Rust family are welcomed permanent residents who take a great interest in the welfare of Thomasville and surrounding area.

Pansy Ireland lived with her mother at Pebble Hill Plantation and followed in her footsteps, working unselfishly to assist those in need and distress. Long before her marriage to Parker Poe she became one of Thomasville's most beloved persons, having moved her citizenship here many years ago. One of her most dedicated interest has been the John D. Archbold Memorial Hospital, which she now serves as trustee.

She was the prime mover in the Thomasville Garden Center and furnished the magnolia trees from Pebble Hill to make the paneling used in the assembly room. Mrs.

Poe purchased the lot upon which stands the famous "Big Oak," that Thomasville is noted for, and created a beautiful park, giving the deed to the Thomasville Garden Clubs. Through her interest, efforts and contributions to the Thomas County Historical Society three excellent volumes have been published on Thomas County history.

It is impossible to enumerate the many worthy endeavors she has sponsored and supported, among them the erection of the Clay Street Y. M. C. A. She is truly one of our most valuable and cherished citizens, and was chosen "Woman of the Year" in 1965. The people of Thomasville and Thomas County will always be thankful that she lived in our midst.

The following picture shows green branches artistically arranged in an imported jardiniere

against the light velvety texture of magnolia paneling, making the Garden Center an attractive gathering place for the women of Thomasville.

The second picture shows the home of Mrs. Parker Poe on Pebble Hill Plantation, in all of its glory. The flowers in full bloom on a

The Thomasville-Tallahassee road, which is one of the most beautiful highways in the south, divides a portion of Foshalee Plantation. Once when I was traveling this stretch I saw a hunting wagon, two dogs on a dead point and two hunters ready to flush a covey of birds. Being a hunter myself I stopped to

clear March day are more beautiful than words can describe.

Harry Payne Whitney became acquainted with the area between Thomasville and Tallahassee through Colonel Lewis S. Thompson and purchased Foshalee Plantation during 1918. Here he built a beautiful hunting lodge and entertained many of his prominent guests.

see what kind of shots they were. I soon learned. The quail flushed and winged their way straight into the direction of my automobile and it was sprinkled with four blasts of bird shots. This taught me the proper etiquette in a situation like this: mind your own business and keep going!

After the death of Mr. Whitney in 1930

his widow, Gertrude Vanderbilt Whitney, retained Foshalee until 1938 when the 11,456 acres were sold to Mrs. Ambrose Clark, whose husband was heir to the Singer Sewing Machine fortune. Mr. and Mrs. Ambrose Clark enjoyed Foshalee under the capable management of Louis B. Campbell. He and his brother Jim A. Campbell were both top game managers.

Louis and Jim told many stories about the visitors who had never held a gun in their hands. One day Louis was standing behind the great opera star, Lucrezia Bori, coaching her on a dove shoot. He would say, "Here comes one on the left. Put up your gun, take off the safety, now shoot." After she shot a box of shells without scoring a hit Louis became discouraged, picked up his own gun and tried to shoot simultaneously with Miss Bori. As the bird fell he cried out, "Good shot, Miss Bori." She put down her gun, looked Louis square in the face and said, "Do not lie to me, I did not shoot."

Louis and Jim Campbell had as much know-how about quail population as anyone on record. During the mating season they often located a hundred or more nests and visited them every day. The story goes that the hen birds became so accustomed to them they were not frightened and allowed Louis or Jim to lift them with a pencil to determine if the eggs were pipped, which is the most dangerous time for vermin.

After the untimely death of Louis Campbell, Mrs. Clark became dissatisfied and sold Foshalee to R. Livingston Ireland and David S. Ingalls. These two men are great friends and their land acquisitions were eventually extended to 29,000 acres in Leon County.

Livingston Ireland is the grandson of Melville Hanna and came up in the Hanna Corporations, serving as President of Hanna Coal Company for many years.

David S. Ingalls is from two prominent Cincinnati families and married Louise Harkness, heiress of much of the estate of William L. Harkness a Standard Oil Company founder.

Mr. Ingalls is a highly decorated naval air ace of World War I and was Assistant Secretary of the Navy for Aeronautics from 1929 to 1932.

George H. Love of Pittsburgh, a longtime friend and business associate of George Humphrey, succeeded Mr. Humphrey as Chairman of the Hanna Company and later became Chairman of the Board of Chrysler Corporation. In 1956 Mr. Love bought 10,000 acres of Sunny Hill Plantation from Governor Edge's widow.

Quoting from a recent book about the Thomasville-Tallahassee section of the country by Clifton Paisley, "From Cotton to Quail:"

"In 1953 Mrs. Jean Hanna Gallien, a granddaughter of Mel Hanna, and her husband A. G. Gallien acquired Mistletoe Plantation in Grady County, Georgia, but with 2,500 acres extending into the northwest part of Leon County. The latest Hanna acquisition is 1,500 acres of Norias Plantation now owned by George M. Humphrey, II, son of Gilbert.

"Following the death of Walter Teagle in 1962, a New York advertising executive C. L. Fitzgerald, acquired much of Norias, but R. L. Ireland acquired part and gave it to his grandson.

"From the Galliens on the west to the Love and Humphrey properties on the east, the lands of the Hannas, their friends and associates now form a block so extensive that one can hardly enter Leon County from the north without crossing it."

The plantations of other Hannas cross the Georgia line. Mrs. Gallien is only a short drive from her grandfather's old place, Melrose, now split into two plantations. One with the same name is owned by her sister Mrs. J. C. Bolton, and another, Sinkola, owned by another sister Mrs. Warren Bicknell, Jr. R. L. Ireland's sister, Mrs. Parker B. Poe, is at Pebble Hill and his son, Robert L. Ireland, III, at Hines Hill not far away.

The Humphreys, Gilbert and George M., II, whose Leon County plantations are three miles apart, are only a short distance from the

Foshalee Lodge.

Milestone Plantation of their father and grand-father, the former Secretary of the Treasury. George Love, in addition to the Leon County acres, has several thousand more in Georgia.

When the Thomasville winter hotels were flourishing, Tallahassee was advertising Leon County as "an unbelievable quail territory" and many northern sportsmen responded. Lake Jackson Hunting Lodge was organized and provided private hunting grounds for several years.

Eventually it was impossible to secure hunting rights because the large tracts of land were being sold, mostly to people from the North,

and the hunting lodges were forced out of business.

One of the first large land purchasers in the Tallahassee section was a Scotchman, Edmund H. Ronalds, in 1887. Then came Clement A. Griscom of Philadelphia who bought Dr. Edward Bradford's Horseshoe Plantation and added many more small and large farms until it reached 10,000 acres. In the early years there were many Negro farm tenants on Horseshoe Plantation but gradually they left, then the land grew into pine forests and Bob White quail became the main crop.

In 1916, after the death of Clement Griscom, his two heirs, Lloyd C. Griscom, and Miss Frances Griscom sold the eastern portion of Horseshoe Plantation to George F. Baker, Jr. Baker was a banker, the son of the founder of New York's First National Bank and a friend of J. P. Morgan. He retained the name Horseshoe for his plantation and made additional land purchases to increase his acreage to 12,640.

Lloyd Griscom established his winter residence on Luna, a four thousand acre plantation on the southern border of Lake Iamonia. Miss Frances Griscom retained a part of Horseshoe east of Luna and gave the name "Water Oak" to her seven thousand acres.

During 1938 a terrible tornado hit Water Oak Plantation and Miss Frances called me for advice concerning the timber. On arriving to inspect the damage I walked for two miles, just about without touching the ground, on the trunks and bodies of trees uprooted and blown down. It had been our worst storm in a hundred years. We learned that the downed trees which still had some root connection with the earth would not quickly blue or deteriorate and we salvaged all of the storm trees.

That work gave me an opportunity to know one of the most interesting women who ever adopted Leon County as her home. Her father was the owner of steamship lines, director of the Pennsylvania Railroad and had many other interests.

Miss Frances was always an energetic, out-of-doors person whose ability on the golf links won her distinction and fame. There were not many golf courses in America at the turn of the century and she learned to play in Scotland on the Northbarrick course. Later she played almost all the East Scotland courses. The Merian Cricket Club, which Miss Frances was always fond of, gave her a lovely silver cup when she won the U. S. Women's Golf Championship in 1900.

The Griscom home overlooked Lake Iamonia and Miss Frances often shot ducks in the morning and spent the afternoon on the hunting wagon watching Mr. Jack Lauder work her favorite dogs.

One morning Miss Frances and her guide were sitting quietly in a boat before daylight waiting for the ducks to fly. They were well concealed in a blind made of dry dog fennels. However, it was a cold freezing day and she became like all hunters, a little nervous before the shooting began. Finally she reached for a cigarette, struck a match which accidentally ignited the dry fennels and in another second her clothing blazed up. Instinctively she dived into the lake—which probably saved her life.

Miss Griscom loved the woods and enjoyed nothing more than having a steady stream of guests to enjoy the hunting, horseback riding and other outdoor activities with her. She was one of the most highly respected and beloved women ever to live in our area.

The formation of the large plantations between Thomasville and Tallahassee began soon after the Civil War and has continued for a hundred years. The tracts often change their shapes and sizes as the owners purchase or sell acreages, trading among themselves or passing the entire plantation on from one generation to the next.

El Destino Plantation was a famous antebellum plantation bought by the late Sheldon Whitehouse of New York. Horseshoe continues in possession of Mrs. George F. Baker. Welaunee, once owned by Mr. and Mrs. Udo M. Fleischmann, is now the property of their nephew John W. Mettler, Jr., of New Jersey. Two plantation owners who became interested in local business enterprises were Colonel Lloyd C. Griscom and John H. Phipps. They bought two news media. Griscom owned the Tallahassee Democrat from 1929 until his death in 1958 and his widow thereafter until 1965. Phipps owns the Thomasville-Tallahassee commercial television station, WCTV.

Thomasville is now known as the "City of Roses." Many of the streets and plots contain beautiful roses, planted and cared for by the town.

100

This picture is a national test plot of Hjort's Nurseries on the highway leading to Valdosta.

CHAPTER ELEVEN

While the foregoing examples of ideal quail-hunting places involve large acreages and often costly management, many small tracts and ordinary farms also have been made highly productive. The whole area is such a natural habitat for Bob Whites that some of them will always be around, even in the unlikely and inaccessible spots. The problem, of course, is to maintain the highest population and the best hunting environment possible.

Starting from scratch in 1960 two of Thomasville's outstanding doctors, Charles H. Watt, Jr., and Huddie L. Cheney, Jr., developed a "wild" place of six hundred acres in Grady County into an excellent hunting preserve. Not overnight, however—it required years, much study and especially hard work, the most of which the doctors did themselves and much of that by hand.

Carefully controlled burning, with very hot fires in selected areas, did much to eliminate heavy scrub brush. Planting small patches of grain and using quail feeders during the critical spring months insured an adequate supply of feed, and in a short time the quail population began to build up. Dr. Watt practically gave up golf because, as he says, he gets more exercise and more satisfaction working in the fields and the woods. He does that at every opportunity, handling an eight-pound tree injector to poison hardwood or planting patches of corn throughout the woods.

The two doctors do not hunt the same course more than once a week and take no more than three birds per covey. Dr. Cheney has a jeep but much of their hunting is done on foot. They examine the crops of killed birds to determine the kind of food being eaten, and Dr. Watt has made a hobby of collecting the seed of wild plants which quail eat. All in all, it has been a successful venture and has brought much joy to two fine families.

The enthusiasm of Dr. Watt and Dr. Cheney and their interest in quail management inspired me to give twenty-five of the plantation managers a dinner at my Myrtlewood camp every year since 1967 for informal discussion. Ideas and practices and discoveries are freely exchanged and all agree that the sessions are interesting and helpful. The managers are experts and keep a good supply of quail on their places, although each one goes about it in a slightly different way. There is no set formula.

Occasionally someone will tell of an original idea or "breakthrough" that succeeded. For instance, while it has been demonstrated that pen-raised quail rarely survive on their own in the wild, T. T. Scott found that hens

Dr. Charlie Watt happily anticipates the whir of wings (left) and (right) takes the dead bird from one dog while the other holds steady.

Dr. Huddie Cheney approaches two of his favorite dogs on point.

released to unmated wild roosters not only had a high survival rate but usually hatched off a covey. He made a recording of the female quail, played it in the woods and would watch one to six or seven roosters hurry in to investigate. He would then release a hen. Do you think the female took up with the first cock bird she saw? No sir! She did as all ladies do, looked them over carefully and made her own selection before marching off to raise a covey of birds. This is now a well proven way to increase the bird supply.

Rather curious developments sometimes come to light. Skunks or polecats, once plentiful to the point of being a nuisance, are rarely if ever seen now, with the result that yellow-jackets have become a great menace. Formerly, the skunks would dig up the underground nests and keep down the yellow-jacket population. One might think anything would be preferable to skunks, but a woodsman will take them to yellow-jackets any time.

Amusing moments in the woods are often recited. Albert Stringer told of running downhill and stepping on a rattlesnake, which he said, "chilled his brains." He returned and killed the snake that spared his life and still wonders if he did right.

While entertaining Senator Herman Talmadge, a splendid marksman, I shot two huge rattlesnakes a few feet away and asked the Senator if he would like to see them. He replied, "No sir, Bob, when I was a small barefoot boy picking short cotton I stepped on a big moccasin and can still feel him."

Doctor Charles Watt told of stepping on a rattlesnake in high grass while wearing low 14″ boots and setting a new broad-jump record.

One of the managers from Alabama said that every man, during the course of his lifetime, deserves to be blessed with at least one good pocket knife, one good woman and one good dog. "I don't know how much you fellows love life, and I never saw you with a knife, but I do know you have all had a

Bolling Jones, III approaching "Dan."

Dr. John Cone walking ahead of "White Knight."

104

John Tyler and T. T. Scott advancing on a covey nailed down in the broom straw by "Little Lou."

good dog."

One might wonder why so many prominent families from all over the United States, able to go anywhere they desired, chose to cast their lot here. Maybe it is the soft air from the Gulf of Mexico, the largest gulf in the world, purified by the trees of a 300,000 acre forest surrounding this section. All of which brings peace and a feeling of well-being into one's life.

Thomasville is located at the frost line where the weather freezes several times during the winter and some frosts occur, destroying many insects and driving the snakes underground. This makes tramping through

the woods a great delight for those who love the outdoors.

Sitting on a hunting wagon or walking behind a pair of dogs as they cast back and forth for quail is probably the greatest pastime on earth. It is not the shooting that counts but the refreshing contact with one of nature's greatest luxuries, the piney woods in South Georgia and North Florida.

Waiting quietly alone in the woods trying to yelp up a wild turkey with a violet leaf, or with a little cypress box no larger than a man's finger and a piece of slate, can be exciting. But the lasting results to a hunter are the long moments he takes for studying God's creation. Listening to the call of birds, admiring the artistic curves of limbs on a hardwood tree which has shed its leaves, watching the wild creatures—all tend to get under a person's skin.

My life has been spent learning how to profitably manage timberland in South Georgia—an endless and ever interesting endeavor. Strange as it may seem, the greatest mistake that I have made is failing to cut the mature trees soon enough to keep them from depressing the small ones. My business is tree-cutting, but I hate to cut trees!

CHAPTER TWELVE

There is no place in America to compare with the area between Thomasville and Tallahassee. It required nearly a hundred years of development to make this section what it is today. Fortunately, the efforts were directed at preserving nature so that the ecology here remains unspoiled. How long it will go on this way depends on the value we place on our environment and the continued efforts of the fifty or more plantation owners whose tracts are shown on the following map.

The land owners not only spend much money maintaining their places but generously contribute to all the worthwhile undertakings for the benefit of the whole community. The John D. Archbold Memorial Hospital alone saves the Thomasville property owners five mills per year.

The hunting of quail and other game birds was so satisfying that the social life of the plantation owners was largely forgotten until 1915. Then, by chance, Col. Lewis S. Thompson, Udo M. Fleischman and Dr. Percy R. Bolton met at the home of Addison F. Hough and decided to organize a field trial.

The first trial was run on Col. Thompson's Sunny Hill Plantation March 2, 1916, and C. M. Chapin's dog was the winner. Miss Frances Griscom's "Calico" took second place.

That was only the beginning, as everyone enjoyed it so much that the Georgia-Florida Field Trial Club was promptly organized with thirty charter members. Every year since, a trial has been run, rain or shine, with the exception of World War II years of 1943-44-45.

The date of the occasion is always fixed a few days before the quail season ends and all the members look forward to getting together and to the event. The trial is run on one of the plantations between Thomasville and Tallahassee or one of the plantations in the Albany area.

Bird dogs are bred to have distinct traits, such as bird sense, wide or close range, eager hunting, merry tail, individual gaits, etc. The trainer teaches them to stand steady to shot and wing, keeping a high head and a straight tail pointing to the sky. The judges select the dog they would rather hunt with that special day.

The following pictures give an idea of the styles of great dogs on point and some scenes of this field trial in action.

The actual running of the Georgia-Florida Field Trial can probably be explained and appreciated better in pictures than in words.

Only a brace of dogs are released at one time, conforming to the custom of a regular day's hunting. It is difficult to manage the members following on horseback, in hunting

Two classy young pointers show their style. The dog on the left is "winding" far-off birds, while the tenseness in the dog on the right leaves little doubt about birds being right in front of his nose.

wagons and jeeps, but everyone seems to get a fair view, even though it takes some doing.

Herschel (Sonny) Clay, Secretary-Treasurer of the Georgia-Florida Field Trial Club, was most helpful in securing many of the pictures of the field trials shown in this book. Mr. Clay is a capable, enthusiastic officer, always working for the interest of the organization.

There are many memorable moments watching the dogs in action. Then, when the noon break comes and the picnic lunches spread on tables, everyone relaxes and enjoys discussing the high points and incidents of the morning's heats. After lunch the club

continued on Page 114

(above) Officials of the 1971 Georgia-Florida Field Trial: *(Left to right):* Gilbert (Bud) Humphrey, President; R. L. Ireland, Chief Marshal; and Gumby Jordon, Judge.

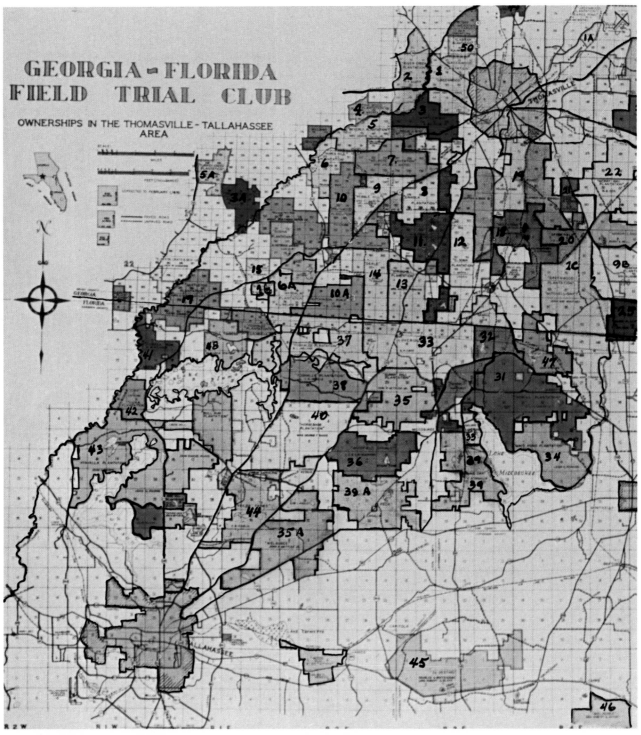

GEORGIA-FLORIDA FIELD TRIAL CLUB

OWNERSHIPS IN THE THOMASVILLE-TALLAHASSEE AREA

PLANTATION		OWNER			
49	Sycamore	Mrs. G. L. Hasty	7	Melrose	Mrs. J. C. Bolton
50	Labrah	R. H. Heinsohn	8	Sinkola	Mrs. Warren Bicknell
1	Greenwood	J. H. Whitney	8-A	Bickaway	Mrs. Warren Bicknell
1-A	Heard's Pond	J. H. Whitney	9	Pebble Hill	Mrs. E. I. Poe
1-B	Boston Place	J. H. Whitney	9-A	Miami	Mrs. E. I. Poe
1-C	Mitchell Place	J. H. Whitney	9-B	Mayhaw	Parker Poe
2	River Creek	T. T. Scott	10	Springwood	Est. of T. C. Chubb
3	Myrtlewood	Balfour Land Co.	10-A	Hutchinson	Est. of T. C. Chubb
3-A	Trulock Place	Balfour Land Co.	11	Longpine	Mrs. W. B. Ford II
3-B	Diston Place	Balfour Land Co.	12	Elsoma	C. Merrill Chapin
3-C	Johnson Place	Balfour Land Co.	13	Springhill	Mrs. Ralph Perkins
3-D	Moore Place	Balfour Land Co.	14	Dekle	Mrs. Royal Firman, Jr.
4	Pinewood	Coastal Lumber Co.	15	Sherwood	H. L. Stoddard, Jr.
5	Beverly	Mrs. George Oliva, Jr.	16	Birdsong	E. V. Komarek
5-A	Turkey Creek	Mrs. George Oliva, Jr.	17	Mistletoe	Mrs. A. Gurnee Gallien
6	Hines Hill	R. L. Ireland, III	18	Milestone	G. M. Humphrey
6-A	Mandalay	R. L. Ireland, III	19	Mill Pond	J. H. Wade, III—Helen G. Perry— E. W. Sedgwick

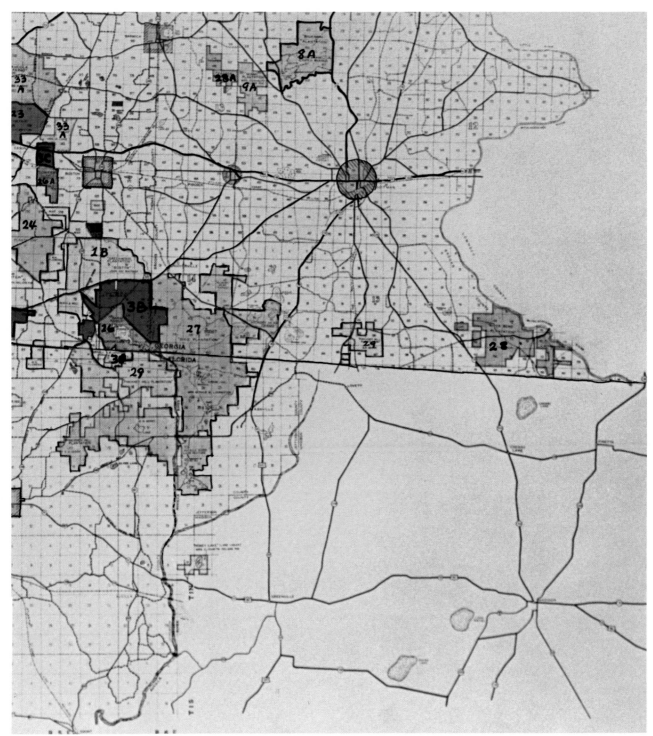

PLANTATION		OWNER				
20	Sedge Field	C. & J. Butler		33-A	Aucilla Farms	G. H. Love
21	Green Ridge	L. B. Harvard		34	May's Pond	Leigh H. Perkins
22	Merryway	W. D. Cox		35	Sunny Hill	J. W. Mettler, Jr.
23	Pine Fair	Charles and Linda Britton, Coburn Britton		35-A	Welaunee	J. W. Mettler, Jr.
24	Seminole	Murchison and Hamilton		36	Woodfield Springs	G. W. Humphrey
25	Ward Place	R. C. Balfour, III		37	Foshalee	R. C. Ireland, Jr.
26	Bar-M Ranch	Ellery Sedgwick, Jr.		38	Foshalee	C. H. Ingalls
26-A	Conifer	Ellery Sedgwick, Jr.		39	Ring Oak	D. S. Ingalls
27	Dixie	Mrs. G. M. Livingston		39-A	Chemonie	D. S Ingalls
28	River Bend	J. H. Thompson		40	Horse Shoe	Mrs. George F. Baker
28-A	Easter	J. H. Thompson		41	Turkey Run	H. W. Nichols
29	Pinckney Hill	E. H. Gerry		42	Luna	Lloyd C. Griscom
30	Merrily	W. H. Flowers		43	Ayavalla	John H. Phipps
31	Norias	C. L. Fitzgerald		44	Velda Farms	C. S. Coble
32	Wildwood	G. M. Humphrey, II		45	El Destino	C. S Whitehouse & Mrs. R. O. Blake
33	Love Ridge	G. H. Love		46	Welaunee	Mrs. Robert G. McKay
				47	Kelly Pond	John W. Hanes
				48	Tall Timbers Research Station	

The handlers get ready to release a brace of dogs.

"My dog's better than your dog!" is sometimes the theme of good-natured banter when members alight from horseback, hunting wagons and jeeps for the noon break.

Members applaud as Mrs. C. Merril Chapin starts forward to receive the Winners Trophy for the 1973 Georgia-Florida Field Trial. *Below:* Mrs. C. Merril Chapin, Mr. and Mrs. Charles M. Chapin, III, William Pearce (handler), and "Elsoma Holly."

holds a short business meeting to elect new officers and make plans for the next field trial.

In the afternoon the trial is completed and the winners announced, thus concluding a colorful day of pleasure. The rivalry is keen with every courtesy observed, and both the owners and handlers can hardly wait to get home before starting to groom the next year's entry, hopefully to win the coveted top honor which is recorded for posterity. Field trials are run over practically all of the United States, but none is like the Georgia-Florida trial.

The plantations require but little looking

Lewis Hall Singletary directs L. B. (Dude) Harvard's attention to a dog on point in the distance. *Below left:* Harvard's fine pointer, Greenridge Joe Mike, winner of the 1974 Field Trial, with handler Rex Hodges.

Mrs. Lewis S. Thompson and Lewis E. Thompson, III, and handler R. D. Barnes, with Winner's Trophies for the 1972 Field Trial.

114

over for one to understand why the owners are so strongly attached to them and to the area—J. H. Whitney once remarked that Greenwood was the last place he would ever get rid of. Little if any less attached to the places are the men who make them tick, the men who take care of the woods work, the farming, the quail propagation, the dog training and so on.

The pictures below were taken of Gordon H. Simmons while training the Greenwood dogs before the hunting season.

The picture on the following page shows Mr. Whitney approaching one of his favorite dogs on point, only a few seconds before a covey of quail explodes from the ideal cover on Greenwood Plantation. The majestic pointer's tail removes any question of a false point.

Katherine (Mrs. Ralph) Perkins of Spring

William H. Flowers, Jr. waits for a covey of Merrily Plantation quail to "level out." The pointer on the right, "Merrily Bud," is a truly outstanding birddog. Under the handling of able trainer Robert Lauder, "Bud" was the winner of the 1970 Field Trial.

Parker Poe swings on a flying target on Pebble Hill Plantation.

115

J. H. Whitney enjoying his favorite activity on his Greenwood Plantation.

Mr. and Mrs. R. L. Ireland, III, their guns safely "on ready," walk in on a point.

Hill Plantation has endeared herself to all the local people.

She is a grand lady who enjoys outdoor sports. These pictures show the ease with which she handles a gun on a covey rise of quail. Eight birds can be seen in flight.

Also, notice how safely her gun is held up while the quail is taken from the Brittany Spaniel.

On a quail hunt "two is company and three

is a crowd," but this is not true with R. C. Balfour, Jr., and R. C. Balfour, III, when they take along their close friend, Dr. John Cone. The only restriction enforced, never over two hunters shoot at one time.

Resting on the hunting wagon is far from hardship because R. T. Dennis, a small black man who walks with a limp and who drives the mules, is so witty and amusing.

The day after the hunting season was over last year I inquired of R. T. if Mr. Bill Vann and his brother Mott enjoyed a good hunt. R. T. said, "Yes Sir, but you know what that big man they call Bill did? He spied a big rattlesnake crawling down a hole, sprung off of de wagon, grabbed it by the tail and jerked it back out. It jest did miss his face."

"What made him do such a thing, R. T.?"
R. T. replied, "Jest lacker knowledge."

On horseback, Sam Ward on the right and Charlie Thompson on the other side of the wagon, always handle the hunt efficiently.

CHAPTER THIRTEEN

During the turn of the century the large lakes between Thomasville and Tallahassee were natural habitats for many species of wild ducks. Today the hunters have increased by tenfold and the same lakes are badly overshot.

The many planted private lakes are now supplying a large portion of the grain and protection to attract and hold the ducks. Without the help of these lakes it is quite possible that we would lose the large flights of ducks visiting us yearly. It would be a step in the right direction for the game departments of Florida and Georgia, as well as the Federal department, to recognize the benefit of putting feed in all our ponds and lakes and to furnish the sound leadership under which they could legally operate, always bearing in mind the protection of the ducks with bag limits strictly observed.

Albert Stringer, one of the best game experts in this area, has advocated the feeding of ducks for a month after the season closes, because of the shortage of natural food. This insures the return of the ducks to their Canadian breeding grounds in a healthy con-

continued on Page 122

Albert Stringer ready to leave for an afternoon's shoot in his duck blind.

Mr. and Mrs. W. H. Flowers, Jr., look pleased as they come in from a morning spent in the duck blind.

Mr. and Mrs. William D. Cox standing on the shore of their beautiful duck pond.

dition. It makes sense.

The following unusual picture of Ringneck ducks was made by P. W. Bryan, Jr. on his small planted lake near Thomasville. The hunting season had closed and the planted grain had been consumed but the ducks lingered on. Therefore, Mr. Bryan began hand feeding them and they came in droves from all directions, eating almost a ton of shelled corn every other day. They were protected, hence the grand picture of Ringnecks, the fastest and tastiest ducks on earth.

The Ringneck weighs one-and-a-half to two pounds and is distinguished from the scaup by his black back with the feathers on the crown being elongated and forming a slight crest.

CHAPTER FOURTEEN

As has been noted, the plantations or game preserves in the Thomasville-Tallahassee area developed as an outgrowth of a thriving winter-resort activity. It started in 1882 when families prominent in social, industrial and financial circles of the nation began spending the winters in this area and became enamored of its natural beauty and the fine hunting it afforded.

The plantations in the Albany, Georgia, area stand next in size and were created or brought about largely by the efforts of one man, Richard Tift, the great grandson of Nelson Tift, who founded Albany in 1836. Richard went into the real estate business in 1924 and became intensely interested in quail hunting, often enjoying the sport with Judge Robert Bingham who owned a considerable tract, called Pineland, in Baker County.

Judge Bingham died during President Roosevelt's first administration while ambassador to the Court of St. James and Mr. Tift bought Pineland Plantation for General and Mrs. Richard Mellon of Pittsburgh, Pennsylvania. Pineland is presently owned by Mrs. Peter Burrell, the former Mrs. Richard Mellon.

Mr. Tift next secured 2,000 acres as a game preserve in Baker County for the famous golfer, Bobby Jones. Over the years he was instrumental in putting together many such places, one of the best known of which was for Robert W. Woodruff, head of the Coca Cola Company in Atlanta, and his friend, Walter White of Cleveland, Ohio. At Mr. White's death the property, known as Ichuaway Plantation, was acquired in its entirety by Mr. Woodruff.

Consisting of some thirty-five thousand acres, Ichuaway is beautifully contoured in pine forests, fields and thickets—everything nature requires to support an abundance of wildlife. Long before the wild turkeys were almost wiped out by a combination of diseases around 1966, and were still very plentiful, I was invited through Bolling Jones, III, to one of Bob Woodruff's famed turkey drives. I arrived at Ichuaway before daylight and was introduced to an array of notables, including General Dwight D. Eisenhower, who had recently returned to the USA and was later to run for the Presidency. It didn't take this country boy long to realize he truly was in "high cotton."

The hunters were placed out of gun range of each other along a dim road which followed the Ichauway Creek as it made a gradual right angle bend. At a signal the beaters started driving the wild turkeys over the stands. General Eisenhower and Edgar Bergen, the famous ventriloquist, occupied

continued on Page 126

124

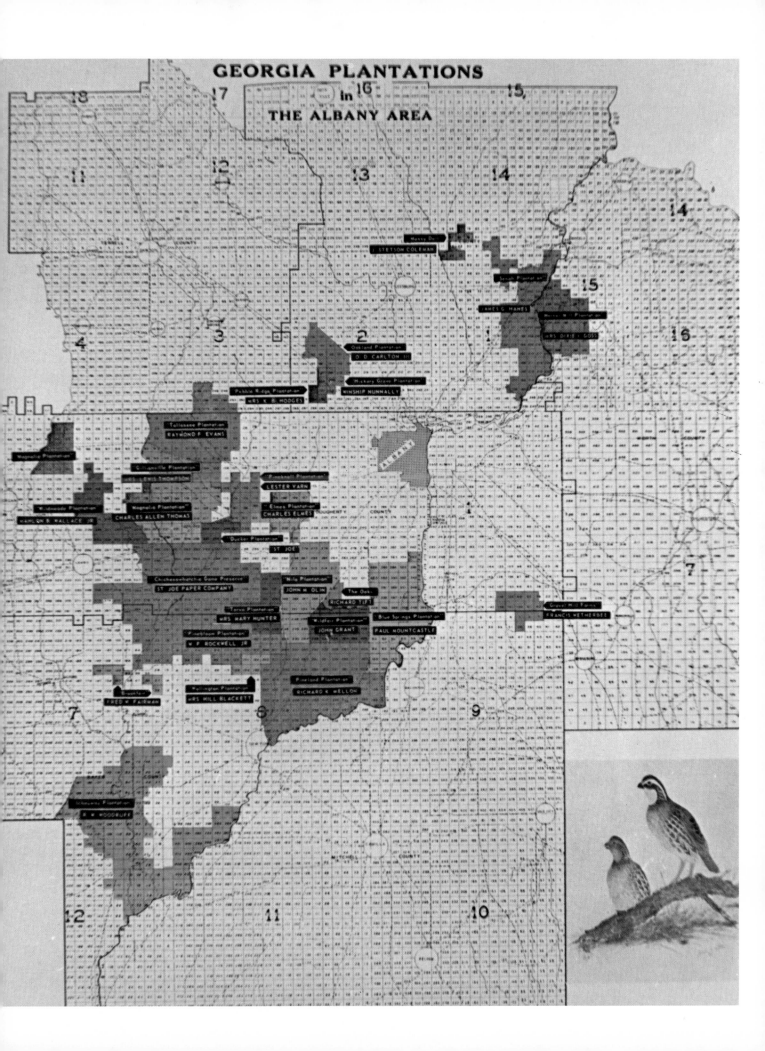

GEORGIA PLANTATIONS
in
THE ALBANY AREA

stands next to each other and as a huge gobbler sailed between them both fired simultaneously and the turkey dutifully fell.

Both hunters hurried to the bird only to learn that each of them had fired. Edgar Bergen picked up the old gobbler, tucked it under his arm and worked its bill as he asked, "Mr. Turkey, who killed you?" The gobbler replied, "You killed me, Bergen." That settled it.

It was a cold day. We returned to the hunting lodge and sat in the sun on the porch while General Eisenhower and Ralph McGill, the Atlanta columnist, told stories about the war. General Eisenhower said his most embarrassing experience occurred while on a

Robert W. Woodruff circling around one of his staunchly pointing dogs. This scenic picture was taken by Charles Elliott of Covington, Georgia. *Right:* Mr. Woodruff relaxing with a "retired" retriever.

126

dress parade. A German airplane came out of nowhere and opened fire, so he dived head foremost into the nearest ditch. When he came out he was covered with mud, medals and all, but continued the parade.

No hunter admires fine dogs and is more attached to his own than Robert W. Woodruff. He maintains a well-kept graveyard and stone markers for the dogs he once enjoyed roaming the woods with.

Mr. Woodruff started the malarial control services for all of Baker County and has helped along countless other worthy causes. He is a gracious host and a wonderful asset to South Georgia.

William C. Potter, President of the Guaranty Trust Company, purchased Blue Springs Plantation. After Mr. Potter's death this property was bought by W. Alton Jones, President of Cities Service. After Mr. Jones'

death it was bought by Paul Mountcastle of Nashville, Tennessee.

Mr. Potter's friend, Mrs. Stafford McClain, developed Wildfair Plantation which was later owned by Alonzo Potter, and then, Winship Nunnally. He later sold to John Grant who owned it for many years. Now Mr. Grant's children own it.

About that same time Dwight Ellis of Springfield, Mass., acquired a large acreage of land in Baker and Dougherty Counties. This property is now owned by John M. Olin of East Alton, Illinois. Known as Nilo Plantation, it has been made one of the finest quail shooting preserves in America. Also Mr. Olin has carried on wide-scope research and has done a magnificent job of advancing practical knowledge of game conservation. This information has been freely shared with other land owners. Those widely attended meetings were

started and conducted for several years single-handedly by Mr. Olin and at his own expense. Now the Georgia Extension Service and the Tall Timbers Foundation have joined with him in sponsoring the meetings.

The picture on the opposite page shows John Olin and his guest, Richard Tift, shooting on Nilo Plantation. The lead dog has a beautiful, sure point.

Probably Mr. Olin's hunting wagon, constructed of aluminum which made it light but still strong, is the best hunting rig anywhere. Mr. Olin, Richard Tift, the writer and the driver are in the wagon.

Mrs. Mary Hunter purchased Tarva Plantation which is now owned by Miss Barbara Hunter and J. Rukin Jelks. This place was first settled by the Tarver family, who built a beautiful ante-bellum home where they lived before the Civil War. The property was first acquired by Russell Algier of Detroit and later sold to Mrs. Hunter who completely restored the old house in its magnificent setting of a grove of live oaks. It is now one of the showplaces of the county.

Adjoining Tarva Plantation is the well-known Pinebloom Plantation which was first purchased by Winthrop Bancroft of Boston,

Massachusetts. Then Hal Price Headley of Lexington, Kentucky, purchased the property, built a magnificent stable and a racetrack for training his racehorses.

Mr. Headley was a great friend of a mutual friend, Major Louis Beard, and I had the great pleasure of entertaining them on my hunting wagon. Major Beard teased Mr. Headley for having entered a horse in the Kentucky Derby more times than any man on earth, but never coming close to winning. Mr. Headley only grinned and remarked that there would be another Derby next May.

Mr. Headley restored the ante-bellum house that originally belonged to Senator Colquitt, Governor of Georgia for two terms after the

Civil War, and who married one of the Tarver daughters. After Mr. Headley's death the 10,000 acre game plantation was purchased by Al Rockwell of Pittsburgh, Pennsylvania, President of Rockwell International.

The Gillionville Plantation is another ante-bellum place presently owned by Mrs. Lewis Thompson who inherited it from General John B. Gordon, a Confederate General in the Civil War and former Governor of Georgia. This large game preserve is located in West Dougherty County and "Lutie," as she is affectionately called, makes her home there. Her father-in-law, Lewis S. Thompson, who owned Sunny Hill Plantation in the Thomasville area is well remembered and his markmanship has become a legend. Lutie raises prize bird dogs and white Labrador retrievers, and takes a great interest in the Georgia-Florida Field Trials.

Adjoining Mrs. Thompson's property is Magnolia Plantation which now belongs to Charles Thomas, President of Monsanto Chemical Company. He has developed Magnolia into a great farm and hunting preserve. It was first purchased by Mrs. Toy Minnix of Ligonier, Pennsylvania, who built the original house. The architect was Edward Jones who is known throughout the country as the leading specialist of colonial-type dwellings. He also supervised the restoration of the Tarva Plantation home, the Gillionville home, Blue Springs Plantation, Nilo, and Mr. and Mrs. Richard Tift's, "The Oaks." He is now doing over a part of the White House in Washington, D. C.

Pine Knoll Plantation also adjoins Gillionville and was first purchased in the early thirties by Tom Daniels of Atlanta. The present owners of this property are John D. Murchison, Fred Hamilton, Frederic C. Church and Charles Hassan.

Just north of Pine Knoll is Tallassee Plantation now owned by Raymond Evans of Cleveland, Ohio, President of Diamond Alkali Company. This property was first pur-

Mr. and Mrs. Richard Tift at home on their 1,500 acre plantation, "The Oaks," south of Albany in Dougherty County.

chased in the late thirties by George Ryan, and after his death was sold to Mahlon Kline of Philadelphia. After his passing it was bought by the present owner. This property has been developed into a fine quail and turkey plantation and also carries on extensive farming and timber production. It is located in Dougherty and Terrell Counties.

James G. Haines of Winston-Salem, North Carolina, President of Hanes Enterprises and his son, Gordon Hanes, purchased Senah Plantation in 1950 and have increased the acreage to 12,000. This property is located in Lee County on the banks of the Flint River ten miles north of Albany. Mr. Hanes was one of the truly great sportsmen of our area and did a great deal for the community in many ways. His grandsons, James G. Hanes, III and Eldridge C. Hanes, are now carrying on the Senah Plantation.

Across the Flint River from Senah is an old plantation known as Mercer Mill, acquired in the late thirties by B. C. Goss of Cleveland, Ohio, and is now owned by his widow, Mrs. Goss. Mercer Mill is in Worth County.

Mossy Dell Plantation consists of 1,500 acres in Lee County. Stetson Coleman started developing this property in the sixties. It is now owned by Earl F. Slick of Winston-Salem, North Carolina.

Home of John M. Olin on Nilo Plantation.

Oakland Plantation is northwest of Albany in Lee County. This 1,500 acre tract was developed by Mrs. John D. Little, later was owned by Mr. Funston of St. Louis and now belongs to O. D. Carlton of Albany.

Wildmeade Plantation is in Calhoun County. This 5,000 acre place was purchased in the fifties by Mahlon Wallace of St. Louis who has developed the property for game and built a fine home.

The land comprising the present large holdings in the Albany area was formerly old, worn out farming properties. It produced very little income and had been mostly taken over by mortgage and insurance companies. The new owners made extensive improve-ments, including the building of better homes for the families who had been living in delapidated old houses without sanitary facilities. The new proprietors started better farming practices, timber reforestation and conservation. They worked and spent money for restoring and conserving of game. They entered into the welfare of just about all local institutions.

Included in the list of plantation owners of the Albany area who built the William C. Potter Community Center are Mr. and Mrs. Richard K. Mellon, Robert W. Woodruff, John Olin, Mahlon Kline, Mrs. Lewis Thompson, Mrs. Mary Hunter and James G. Hanes, among others.

Members of the Georgia-Florida Field Trial Club in front of the William C. Potter Community Center, Albany.

CONCLUSION

This, then, is my outdoor world. It is only a small portion of the earth's vast surface but its likeness is not to be found anywhere. I have loved every outing I've spent in these woods and fields, on the streams and lakes— and I still do, for by God's blessing I fish, hunt and play golf about as ever. Truly, the Lord is my Shepherd.

If I were to be granted one last wish it would be that this unspoiled land might stay unspoiled. I would like for my children and their children, and all children for that matter, to be able to fill their lungs with its clean, soft air, to watch its wildlife, to listen to its birdsong, to the yelping of turkeys, the distant scream of a hawk, the plaintive, muted cooing of doves high up in the tall pine trees.

There will be changes, of course. I have seen many changes in my lifetime, and yet, much of the area is still the same as when the Indians lived here. This despite the huge portion which has been made productive of food and fibre for man's use, and so harmoniously have conservation and productivity been managed that wildlife is even more plentiful today than in the time of the Indians.

It is most heartening to note that people all over the nation and much of the world are becoming concerned about living peaceably with the environment and conserving the earth's resources. Ecologists from the world over gather here at the Tall Timbers Research Station's environmental symposiums to learn and exchange ideas, and especially to "field study" practical conservation on a scale that is probably unrivaled anywhere.

My generation has seen the flowering of man's God-given "dominium over the earth and all that is therein." Plainly, reckless use of this gift will exterminate all living creatures, including man himself, from the face of the earth. Just as plainly, man can get along with and live with his environment so that all creatures survive and all thrive. The choice is his to make.

My aim has been to leave the land that was entrusted to my care in better condition than I found it. I hope I succeeded. I hope too that I will pass on to future generations, along with the land, that same aim and dedication.

Robert C. Balfour Jr.